Oriental Dance Curriculum

Oriental Dance Curriculum

Beginner to Multilevel

A Complete Guide for the Belly Dance Teacher

By Katayoun Hutson

Published by Mosaique LLC, 2015

Sterling, VA USA

Copyright © 2015 by Katayoun Hutson

All rights reserved. This book or any portion thereof may not be reproduced or used in any manner whatsoever without the express written permission of the publisher except for the use of brief quotations in a book review.

Printed in the United States of America

First Printing, 2015

ISBN 978-0-692-43374-4

Mosaique LLC
Publishing Division
1323 Shepard Drive, Suite D
Sterling, VA 20164

www.RaqsMosaique.com

Editing by Lora R. Bates, M.Ed.
ESOL Department Chair, Oakton High School
Fairfax County Public Schools

Interior photographs by Laura Walz

Cover design by Laura Walz and Adrian Hutson

Artwork and design concepts by Adrian Hutson

*Dedicated to my mother, who decided I needed real dance lessons.
I think about you everyday.*

Acknowledgements

To Janeeda… I am forever grateful for your guidance and support in my first dance experience.

To my family, Charles and Kavon…thank you for putting up with my craziness and giving me the space to do what I need to do. Adrian, thank you for your amazing artwork and creative ideas.

To my Eshvehettes, Ayperi, Amira, Jennifer, Shukufeh, Sitara and Suzana…thank you for believing in me. Your encouragement and friendship mean so much.

To Aunt Rocky, your influence and encouragement have inspired and educated so many. I am so fortunate to be among them.

And to my students, past and present…. you inspire me everyday.

About the Author

Katayoun was born in Tehran, Iran and grew up in Virginia Beach, Virginia where she began studying Classical Egyptian belly dance while competing in a teen scholarship pageant.

Today, she is best known for her interpretations of Egyptian folklore and the Persian dances of her heritage. Her expressive dance style has been described as "elegant and earthy," "powerful yet subtle," with "perfect musicality and interpretation."

An innovative, dedicated and enthusiastic teacher, she has taught weekly classes to students of all ages and backgrounds since 1999, accumulating over 8,000 instructional hours as a classroom teacher and studio instructor. She has continued her dance education with over 350 hours of advanced and specialized training with nationally and internationally acclaimed artists. Her teaching experience includes many opportunities to educate diverse audiences about the beauty and benefits of Middle Eastern dance.

While her focus is on folkloric and regional dance and music, her training includes modern Oriental, Arabic tabla technique and ATS (American Tribal Style belly dance). She currently trains in ballet. Other education and training include a bachelor's degree in French from George Mason University and graduate coursework in education, curriculum and instruction through the University of Virginia. A Thespian with training in the dramatic arts, her performance roots took hold in high school and college theater.

From her early childhood in pre-revolutionary Iran, to coming of age as an Iranian-American amidst the 1980 hostage crisis, in adulthood she reconciled her two worlds through music and dance. Her journey in dance began in 1988 at the age of 17 with a generous and kind teacher by the name of Janeeda Phillips, who taught the classical cabaret style of the era. Like so many others, Katayoun felt an instant connection to the music and movements. At the time, she never imagined dance would become a life-long endeavor, a passion she would pursue through every phase of her life.

Before belly dance would capture the imagination of Americans in the early 2000's as the hottest new fitness trend, practitioners of the art would struggle to reconcile the archaic misconception of belly dance as the "dance of seduction." As a young instructor and new entrepreneur at the turn of the 21st century, Katayoun was personally involved in a high-profile controversy surrounding the dance in the small resort town of Destin, Florida, where her students were banned by the mayor from performing in a community celebration. The incident was scandalous and newsworthy for this small town, inspiring headlines such as "Belly Dancers, Too Wild." It was during this time the seeds for her teaching philosophy and performance style were planted.

The hard and sometimes controversial lessons learned in that first year of teaching, along with her background as an educator the classroom, led her to create a dance format and curriculum for teaching Oriental dance.

Upon relocating to the Washington, DC area in 2000, she began a successful full-time career as an elementary school French teacher at a prestigious private school while maintaining a schedule of dance training, teaching and performing. She has garnered a reputation as one of the most respected dancers in the area, by promoting teaching standards and breadth of knowledge through her classes, performances and teacher-training programs.

Between 2001 and 2005 in her role as an event producer, she and her students initiated and coordinated several benefit events, which raised over $10,000 combined for local and international charities, including the high profile campaign, Dance from the Heart for Oxfam's Tsunami Relief Fund. In 2008, Katayoun helped form the professional performance group, Troupe Eshveh, Northern Virginia's premiere folklore Middle Eastern dance ensemble.

In 2010, she was one of 25 dancers selected from around the world to participate in the first season of Project Belly Dance, the search for America's Top Belly Dancer, a competition and reality show.

An entrepreneur and community leader, she has served on the boards of WAMEDA (Washington-Area Mid-East Dance Association) as an officer, and Tiraz Dance Network as a founder. Currently, she serves as CEO and Artistic Director of Mosaique Center for Cultural Arts in Sterling, Virginia, an organization she founded in 2009, where she teaches 10-14 classes per week to adults and kids of all ages, abilities and backgrounds.

She is an accomplished performer, sought-after for her creative artistry and cultural authenticity, which she weaves seamlessly into her professional standards and teaching ethics. She believes that regardless of dance style, when music, culture and movement are connected to create dance performance, the dancer and her audiences are fully engaged and continuously inspired.

Katayoun performs for community events, exclusive gatherings and select audiences as a soloist and with Troupe Eshveh. She lives in Northern Virginia with her husband of over 20 years. They are proud parents of two talented artists pursuing higher education and careers in music and visual arts.

Katayoun's Raqs Mosaique - www.KatayounDance.com
Mosaique Center for Cultural Arts in Sterling, VA - www.Mosaique-Center.org
Raqs Mosaique Belly Dance Teacher Training - www. Raqsmosaique.com
Twitter.com/KatayounDance
Facebook.com/katayoundance

"I've learned that people will forget what you said, people will forget what you did, but people will never forget how you made them feel." ~ Maya Angelou

Contents

Introduction 7

Part I
Foundations & Essentials

1. Curriculum Overview 13
2. Movement Vocabulary 21
3. Music Fundamentals 35
4. Layering & Build-Up Method 41
5. Class Structure, Sequence & Pace 47

Part II
Thematic Units & Lesson Plans

1. Introduction 65
2. Fall Session: Foundations in Folklore 67
3. Winter Session: Music & Choreography 117
4. Spring Session: Performance Skills 169
5. Summer Session: Specialty Topics 221

Resources 229

Foreword

"I WISH SHE HAD WRITTEN IT SOONER"
By Morocco (C. Varga Dinicu)

I first "met" Katayoun Hutson online in early December 1999, when she wrote to the best chat list on Middle Eastern and North African dance (med-dance@world.std.com) for help. Dancers, teachers, students and aficionados posted questions, information, misinformation, theories, and fantasies. It was moderated by Eileen Bauer, a truly ecumenical computer professional.

Katayoun, originally from Iran, lived and taught Oriental dance in Florida as a way of sharing ethnic dances of the Near and Middle East. She loved and respected that part of her culture and her students danced with class and pride. They performed at special events and were scheduled to dance in the Destin Community Center's Christmas tree-lighting ceremony/show.

Why did she need help? Here it is, straight from the Northwest Florida Daily News:

A dance style used in celebration and family gatherings for centuries was deemed inappropriate for children and removed from Destin's Christmas tree-lighting ceremonies Thursday.

Middle Eastern dance instructor Katayoun Hutson was told Thursday afternoon her dance class could not perform at the Christmas festivities here Thursday night. The city's Recreation Director Muri Kersanac made the phone call. "That was the hardest thing I've ever had to do here," Kersanac said Friday.

As recreation director, Kersanac had invited all the dance classes taught at the city's Community Center, including Hutson's, to participate in the festivities. "I never even thought it would conflict," Kersanac said.

In addition to teaching Middle Eastern dance for eight months at the Destin Community Center, Hutson volunteered with the children's summer camp at the Destin Community Center. That class, Kersanac said, is one of the children's favorites.

"She's a professional dancer; there's nothing dirty about it," Kersanac said.

Everything, from the use of bells in the dance to the colors of Hutson's authentic costume - red and green - would have fit right in with the ceremonies, Kersanac said. But a mayor outranks a recreation director.

> Destin Mayor Ken Beaird didn't see the program for Thursday night's celebration until that day. When he did, he was surprised to see belly dancing on it. Apparently he was not alone.
>
> "I had a concerned citizen call me and he said it was not appropriate," Beaird said. "I agreed with him."
>
> Although he's never seen Hutson or her class perform, Beaird was concerned that the dance style would be inappropriate for the many very young children who would be attending and performing that night, and had Kersanac remove it from the lineup.

Of course, I (and several others) wrote to Mayor Beaird to correct his misconceptions and educate him about this joyous ethnic dance, one fit for the whole family. Would he rethink his negative position?

To give him his due, he answered my letter, explaining that his experience with this dance was when he was in the military and what he saw was not fit for children. Despite a second letter from me explaining that bar owners catering to male military trade were not interested in presenting family entertainment, which was what Katayoun's dancers were, he did not change his mind.

Katayoun and I remained Internet friends and now she has written an excellent book and honored me with her request to write its introduction. I asked for and received an advance copy, we e-mailed back and forth about a few small technicalities and I am very pleased to be able to recommend it highly – and not just to teachers of Raqs Sharqi/ Oriental dance / "belly" dance – this is an excellent aide for every dance teacher.

She wrote to me:

> *"Emphasizing the importance of musical and cultural understanding is a hallmark of my curriculum that I've developed over the past 15 years, and I credit you for that influence and inspiration. My mission ever since our first Internet encounters on the MED-List, after that horrid experience, has been to not only educate the public, but dancers and instructors as well, to promote breadth of knowledge and standards of teaching and learning.*
>
> *There are a few books and many training programs on "how to teach", but there are no books on "what to teach". Even school teachers trained in the art and science of pedagogy, go into the classroom with a curriculum already in place. Not so for the Oriental dance teacher. A cohesive curriculum that can be widely used is very much needed. I believe I am offering that."*

Indeed, she is! I wish she had written it sooner – it would have saved me so much trial and error time. Her lesson plan outlines are easy to use "as is" or adjust to your own curriculum, preferred movement vocabulary and names for the movements.

There are "boxed" teaching tips at the end of each class outline - I especially like the reminder to thank the students for coming to class, and her ethical approach in general. Stage directions are included in her later choreographies. There are "find the Doum" exercises and suggestions for variety, plus folk-ish things for variety in summertime classes. There is much to like about this book! Enjoy!

Morocco *is considered the leading authority in the field of Middle Eastern dance in the U.S., Canada, and abroad. With over 50 years of researching, assimilating, lecturing, performing and teaching classes and master seminars in the U.S., Europe, Asia and the Middle East, she has received numerous awards and accolades in this field. Her articles have been published internationally in dance journals as well as medical and feminist publications since 1965.*

Introduction

When I was "growing up" as a dancer in the 1990's, the Internet had taken off and belly dance was just coming out of a major slump after the boom of the 1960's and 70's. My first belly dance lessons were held in a rented basement classroom with mirrors. Looking back, the fact that it had mirrors was amazing. In fact, all of the classes I took during that time, in every town I lived, were held in rented spaces or were taught through the local recreation centers.

There were hardly any belly dance studios or schools, like we see in commercial spaces today. We also didn't have the vast number of events and resources that are now available. Other things that were missing were structured levels and a codified system of learning. Every class was different. Every teacher taught a different way. The one commonality I experienced was the multilevel classroom. There is still not a universal system (and that's *okay* in my opinion), but we have come a long way in the organization and codification of the dance.

When I started dancing, it was definitely a different time. Belly dance was experiencing a downturn in popularity (which it would regain in the 2000's), and many teachers consolidated all their students into one class. There were simply not enough students to create viable and cost-effective classes for each level.

In my first belly dance class, I was the only beginner student. I learned right alongside the troupe members. Later, in another town, in another state, I joined a class with a similar format. I had no formal experience with dance schools of any kind, so I formed an impression that this is how classes were run everywhere. Beginner and experienced, even professional-level students would learn together in the same class.

As a teen in this first belly dance class, I was taken under the wing of a community of welcoming women. Instead of having one teacher, I had a family of mentors. At the end of each class, when it was time for the troupe to rehearse the choreographies, I had to sit out and watch. I was amazed and enchanted every time. I thought, "Will I ever learn to dance like that?" Although, when it was time for me to jump in and learn the choreography, I was intimidated. Of course, I stumbled badly. Nevertheless, it is a memory I cherish.

Many years later when I found myself teaching, I began to adapt the multilevel model in my own classes and eventually expanded it. It has taken many shapes and forms over the years, and it continues to evolve. However, the fundamental concepts I developed in those first few years of teaching have proved to be the essential foundation for teaching all varieties of classes, as well as all levels and audiences.

The multi-level class model has become the signature characteristic of my format. At one point, I tried to divide my classes into levels. After a while, I realized that I was driven to accommodate the interests and needs of my students' levels of experience, more than by the criteria of the course. I easily resumed to what felt natural, and my curriculum began to take on new life. It was clear I was filling a need and I found the multilevel model worked the best. It was simple to teach and simple to learn.

When done right, teaching belly dance as a cultural-based art form, in a multilevel format, offers advantages and solutions over the conventional levels-based instruction of Western dance schools.

- Experienced students continually polish the basics as they develop new skills and knowledge.

- Beginner students immediately become part of a community of mentors and role models

- No attrition of students due to low enrollment in a particular level. Consolidate students into one multilevel class.

- Utilizing horizontal and vertical skill-building strategies keeps students at all levels engaged and motivated, especially students whose primary goals are simply to live happier and healthier.

Oriental dance is more than movements. It is an embodiment of a unique musical form and cultural expression. For this reason, the art, craft, and science of teaching belly dance must incorporate more than mechanics of movements. Movement without expression and artistry is just movement with no meaning.

Ask any belly dancer who has been involved in the art for many years, why the continued fascination? I guarantee you will get answers like, "There is so much to learn!" Obviously, we are not talking about the moves. It means that Oriental dance is a manifestation of a vast array of cultural flavors and artistic influences that simply cannot be explored through the practice of movement alone. The movements are simply the vehicle to the understanding and embodiment of that expression. It is a rich and complex art that demands a multi-disciplinary approach. The art of Oriental dance may be complex. Teaching it should not be.

I often compare learning dance to language learning. First, you learn the alphabet, and then you put the letters together to make words. When you've learned some words, you begin to make sentences, and eventually paragraphs of thoughts and expressions.

Learning dance is very similar. First you must learn the alphabet of movement - muscle engagement. Then you put them together to learn words or vocabulary of movements, such as hip circle and figure eight. Then you learn to make sentences or combinations of movements and steps. Finally, you can write a full essay or choreography comprised of many combinations organized in musical phrases, or paragraphs.

I love the analogy of dance to language because dance is a language of expression, and in my other life, I was a language teacher. The other commonality between language learning and dance, especially Oriental dance, is that when learning a foreign language, there is an essential cultural element. Without this cultural context, a true understanding and appreciation of the language and dance will remain elusive and vague with a limited potential for advancement.

When I began my teaching career in the school classroom, designing a curriculum was not often part of the job. Usually, there was a curriculum already in place, developed and written by experienced educational leaders in the field. I ended up writing one anyway, since my school did not have an adequate one for my program. In many ways, my development as a classroom teacher and a dance teacher were parallel.

Unless you belong to a studio that has developed its own curriculum, when you start out as a belly dance teacher, you're on your own. Even experienced instructors often piece-meal lessons together from forums and Internet sources. Since the parts and pieces come from different standards and perspectives, rarely will they come together as a credible and cohesive whole. This is a challenge most belly dance teachers accept and take on. Until now, there was not a cohesive curriculum. Until now, you had to beg, borrow, and steal or write your own curriculum. So I did. Now I share it with you.

I've used this format successfully in all my classes for over 15 years. Teachers in my mentoring program often ask how I effectively teach multilevel classes. I've compiled the latest manifestation of my curriculum in this book. The format is specific in some areas and general in other areas. This is done intentionally to give you structure and organization as well as flexibility to develop your own ideas.

When followed with the same thoughtful process used to create this book, and sprinkled with your own creativity, this curriculum guide will give you the tools you need to teach successful multilevel classes for years to come.

How to Use This Curriculum Guide

You may teach the material in this curriculum in a variety of ways to fit your scheduling and class needs.

There are three ways you can use this curriculum guide:

1. **Select individual lesson plans from any unit.** This is a good option if you teach drop-in classes. Mix and match lessons to create your own themes and units.

2. **Divide the curriculum and accompanying sessions into class levels, such as Level 1, Level 2, and Level 3.** You will need to determine which theme best corresponds to each level. Use your best judgment to determine what you think will work best for you and your students.

3. **Teach this curriculum in progressive sessions in the order it is presented.** Start with the current or upcoming season and teach the sessions one after the other. By the time you get through all the sessions and lesson plans, you will have many ideas of your own, and will rely less and less on this book.

Whichever option you choose, you will need to keep in mind different learning objectives according to the experience level of the students.

Supporting materials such as online videos and DVD's, may be available on my teacher training website, **www.raqsmosaique.com**, and as part of my seminar and workshop content.

I wrote this book specifically for the belly dance teacher, whether new and seeking some guidance, or experienced looking for new ideas. It is meant to be used in the art, practice and teaching of Oriental dance. It is not meant to sit neatly on a shelf collecting dust, rather it is meant to get beat up from constant use.

I encourage you to mark it up, highlight it, color in it, express your reaction (even if you disagree), roll it up, carry it around, and splay it in front of you to reference as you teach. That is how I imagine this book being used and not to be preserved as a coffee table fixture. My hope is that this book helps you thrive and soar in your teaching and dance endeavors.

Part I

Foundations & Essentials

1

Curriculum Overview

A successful dance program is based on a strong foundation of clearly defined learning goals and objectives, a diverse array of activities, and a good understanding of the development needs and interests of the students.

The purpose of this curriculum guide is two-fold:
1) To provide goals and objectives for the teacher and the students.
2) To promote teaching standards and breadth of knowledge in the art of Oriental dance.

This multilevel curriculum program will primarily address the needs and learning goals of beginner and continuing recreational students. While the themes and topics may be used to teach intermediate and advanced level classes, you will need to modify the objectives and lessons to address the performance goals of more advanced students.

In education, the curriculum is the "what." What are the topics and the depth of information to which students will be exposed? What is the purpose of presenting the content to students, i.e. what are the learning goals and objectives of the program?

Pedagogy is the "how." How will the content of the program be presented? How will the students experience the topic and information to which they are exposed? And finally, how will students and teachers know they have achieved the learning objectives?

With tips and general guidelines are offered on the "how' or teaching strategies, this guide will primarily address the "what" or content of the Oriental dance course. I also share golden nuggets of "Teaching Tips" that I have learned in many years of experience, teaching many different students.

Much of learning how to teach is actually doing it, and documenting your thoughts and observations. When you are new to teaching, you will need to rehearse and time your class presentation. With experience, you will learn what works well for you and what does not. Regardless of experience, it is important to continue being a student yourself, and occasionally try new methods, styles, techniques, and strategies.

Students learn lots of movements that help them build a vertical foundation. Perhaps they are able to perform movements and combinations, but have difficulty moving toward mastery and artistry. To help them build horizontal skills with a broader range of experience and knowledge, thoughtful planning is required.

This curriculum and accompanying units will help students achieve a higher level of success. Instruction will be more effective if it focuses on dance objectives students will achieve, rather than solely on lists of movements, combinations, and choreographies to be taught by the teacher.

This curriculum package will guide you step-by-step to teach a year-long beginner in a multilevel belly dance program. Presented in seasonal thematic units, each unit is divided into two six-week sessions with separate but compatible plans for each season: fall, winter, spring and a special summer session. Suggestions for music and playlists are also included.

While designed to be readily accessible to beginner dancers, the topics and techniques are perfect for teaching multi-level classes. These are classes where you have a mix of new beginner and more experienced returning students in the same class.

While the curriculum is organized as a year-long plan, there are many possibilities to expand and vary each theme's movements, music and choreography. It is designed to keep students interested and motivated with different topics while they continue to polish the basics and advance their skills throughout the year.

The sessions are presented in thematic units that address the learning objectives of the curriculum using both vertical and horizontal skill-building strategies. The learning objectives encompass the three elements of cultural dance proficiency:

1) Technique

2) Music & Cultural Context

3) Artistry

Technique	Music & Culture	Artistry
Muscle Engagement	Rhythms	Essence or Flavor
Body Alignment	Instruments	Presentation
Movement Dynamics	Timing	Aesthetics
Transitions	Meaning of movements	Interpretation

Session plans are provided in six-week increments, which you can modify and arrange for eight, ten or twelve-week programs.

About Goals & Objectives

There are two sets of behaviors or goals and objectives addressed in this curriculum guide. The **Learning Goals** are student behaviors or the desired result. The **Teaching Objectives** are the teacher's actions, which help students achieve the learning goals. In general, the terminology of 'goal' and 'objective' may be interchangeable. The idea is that there are two sets of desired behaviors in the training process; the teacher's instruction and guidance, and the students' behavior demonstrating understanding and proficiency.

Curriculum Learning Goals

- Students will become familiar with the fundamental movements and concepts of Middle Eastern dance forms as a performance art. Regional and performance styles introduced may include Egyptian Raqs Sharki (Oriental), Persian dance, and a variety of folkloric steps. These traditional forms provide the foundation of the movement vocabulary and aesthetic concepts of modern Oriental belly dance.
- Students are expected to become more proficient and confident in the basic movements and steps throughout the year.
- Students are encouraged to attend student and professional performances in the community and to network with other dancers.
- Throughout the year, returning students will continue to polish technique and gain a more detailed understanding of aesthetics and concepts, such as music interpretation and cultural expression. When appropriate, performance dynamics will be emphasized with increasing attention to detail.

While you can teach any unit in this curriculum to students who have no previous knowledge, the learning objectives and behaviors will vary depending on their level of experience.

Level 1 Students (0 to 3 months experience)

- Demonstrate mechanics of proper form and technique with a focus on muscle engagement and body alignment through self-correction, teacher-correction, and reinforcement
- Identify the "Doum" and "Tek" of rhythms introduced
- Following the teacher, perform basic movements with smooth transitions to create combinations
- Perform movements and combinations with increased accuracy and confidence
- Identify the geographic roots and cultural contexts of modern belly dance

Level 2 Students (3 to 6 months experience)

- Demonstrate mechanics of proper form and technique through self-correction when guided by the teacher
- Identify one or two rhythms and choose appropriate movements to mark the accented beats
- Following the teacher, perform dance sequences and combinations with increased accuracy and confidence
- Utilize the appropriate vocabulary to identify and describe belly dance origins/geographic locations, and cultural contexts

Level 3 or Continuing Students (6 to 12+ months experience)

- Demonstrate proficiency in the basic movement vocabulary of Oriental dance styles
- Perform movements and combinations with increased accuracy and confidence
- Identify three common dance rhythms and choose appropriate movements or combinations to interpret them
- Independently perform a short choreographic sequence learned in class
- Utilize the appropriate vocabulary to identify Middle Eastern dance geography and cultural contexts
- Distinguish between interpretive or fusion belly dance and authentic cultural styles
- Perform a dance sequence or choreography in front of an audience (optional)

Skills & Standards

The learning behaviors of students will be different depending on their level of experience and training. Individuals have different needs, limitations, goals and self-expectations. The length of time recommended for each level is approximate based on many teachers' observations and experiences and is merely to give you an idea how long it may take to integrate the specific skills. However, there are typical learning behaviors at different levels of experience, which will help you establish standards for the skills level of the classes you offer.

Whether some students exhibit these learning behaviors sooner or later than average, is largely based on motivation, interests and goals, not necessarily on ability. With this in mind, students who do not aspire to perform should be given the same opportunities to learn about music, choreography and performance skills if it enriches their experience and offers opportunities for improvement.

A beginner level dancer (0 to 1 year training), is discovering a variety of styles and cultures associated with Oriental dance. The beginner dancer needs more experience, reinforcement and repetition in order to master the foundation material in the curriculum.

- Needs constant reinforcement, repetition and encouragement to properly perform the fundamental movement vocabulary

- Typically enjoys variety of music and movements, but needs guidance and direction to apply the movement vocabulary in context

- Struggles with use of space and transitions, but enjoys the challenge if presented in the context of choreography or for another specific purpose

- Enjoys discovering the variety of dance styles and cultures associated with Middle Eastern (Oriental) dance

An intermediate level dancer (1 year + training), strives to polish movement vocabulary and combinations on a more refined and complex level. The intermediate dancer is very proficient in properly performing the fundamental movement vocabulary of Oriental dance, but needs consistent practice to maintain and build on those skills.

An intermediate dancer is aware of and is exploring a variety of dance styles and concepts within the movement vocabulary of Middle Eastern/North African dance.

- Has a solid understanding of the foundational movement vocabulary, , but needs to polish and refine regularly to advance and grow

- Yearns for new contexts and combinations to continue refining musicality and movement skills

- When instructed, is able to embellish basic movement vocabulary with layering and variations for different styles of dance and music

- Is aware of and enjoys a variety of Oriental, Folkloric and Fusion dance styles

- Has a working knowledge of Middle Eastern/Arabic Music and rhythms

- Is hungry to expand repertoire of choreography and improvisational skills

An advanced level dancer (3 to 5 years+ progressive training), has discovered a vision of a personal dance style which he or she strives to fulfill. This level of dancer has developed a critical eye for detail in his/her own performance as well as others' and recognizes, and appreciates new opportunities to study specialty and specific styles.

- Has mastered fundamental movement vocabulary and continues to polish and practice for further advancement

- Applies and modifies class material independently to perform as a soloist with artistry, showmanship, and musicality

- Has solid understanding of common dance rhythms and corresponding movements and combinations

- Enjoys and seeks opportunities to explore and study a diverse repertoire of stylistic and ethnic dance forms

- Is able to perform and create choreography and can improvise to fill gaps of knowledge

2

Movement Vocabulary

The movement vocabulary is the foundational material required to create dance. This chapter describes in detail the common foundational springboard that all dancers need to build their skills, no matter what level.

There are 10 foundational components or building blocks of Oriental belly dance. They will all be addressed in different thematic units over the course of the curriculum.

1. **Isolations:** Muscle contractions
2. **Foundation Movements:** Weight-centered and weight-shifted body articulations
3. **4/4 Shimmies:** Oblique-driven, quad-driven
4. **Steps:** Weight shifts and traveling
5. **Arms:** Movements, transitions and poses or frames
6. **Pivots & Turns:** Foot positions, balance and body carriage
7. **Rhythm, Timing & Coordination:** 3/4 shimmies and step variations
8. **Directions & Dynamics:** Floor patterns and use of space
9. **Layering:** Simultaneous multiple movements and/or dynamics
10. **Choreography and Improvisation:** Musicality and artistry

Each fundamental component builds on the previous to progress from basic movement proficiency to advanced skill building.

Categorized by body region and skill sequence, foundational elements are addressed in the curriculum based on the theme of the unit. While each unit will focus on very specific themes and skills, we will touch on some variation of all the foundational components in every unit.

For example, each unit includes steps and turns or pivots. However, only those steps that pertain to the unit theme are included. Each teacher may add his or her own variations to the mix.

Oriental Dance Positions: Arms and Feet

While muscle isolations and body movements are the core movement vocabulary of Oriental dance, defining the positions of the arms and feet will help prepare students for balance and coordination in performing steps, traveling, turns and transitions. I have designated numbered positions similar to ballet terminology. You can call these positions whatever you like, as long as you and your students can remember them.

First position

Arms: Rounded or extended, framing the body.

Feet: Parallel, weight distributed evenly.

Second position

Arms: Extended symmetrically or asymmetrically

Feet: Weight is on one foot; other foot is extended to the side. This position is often called Arabesque.

Second position symmetrical arms

Second position asymmetrical arms

Third position

Arms: Rounded or extended symmetrically or asymmetrically, framing the body.

Feet: Parallel, weight is on one foot, heel of the other foot is lifted. This position is often seen as the classic belly dance pose.

Third position rounded symmetrical arms *Third position extended asymmetrical arms*

Fourth position

Arms: Extended out or up in V pose.

Feet: Weight is on one foot; the other is extended forward.

Fourth position arms extended out   *Fourth position arms extended up in V pose*

Fifth position

Arms: Extended symmetrically or asymmetrically.

Feet: Parallel, weight is on one foot, other foot is extended back with heel lifted. This is another variation of second position Arabesque.

Fifth position arms extended symmetrically

Fifth position arms extended symmetrically

Arm Frames and Paths: Arms may be extended, rounded, symmetrical or asymmetrical. Movement patterns are often circular, transitioning from the center of the body to change positions.

Arms extended to arms rounded

Asymmetrical arms to V pose

Foundational Movements and Steps

An ***isolation*** is a contraction of muscles. By itself, an isolation may or may not be used as a dance move to interpret music. More often, an isolation is a component of a basic movement or articulation. Typically, movement isolations use two sets of muscles, which surround the body part you want to isolate or move.

A ***movement or articulation*** is a sequence or combination of isolations performed with the muscles in the torso. Movements (and isolations) may be performed with body weight shifted or centered in a variety of dance positions. The terms *movement* and *articulation* may be used interchangeably in this curriculum guide.

A ***step*** is a shift of weight from one foot to the other, and allows for traveling and other use of space.

Presenting ***movements***, ***isolations***, and ***steps*** as separate concepts will help students build their skills from a strong foundation that incorporate every part of the body. This format will help develop body awareness and coordination. As foundational components are sequentially added in the Layering and Build-up Method, you will continually develop interesting combinations and dance dynamics.

Lower Body
Isolations

Abdominal contraction: A contraction of abdominal muscles: Lower abdominal contraction (pelvic floor) and middle/upper abdominal contraction.

Abdominal release: The opposite of a contraction, a release of the lower abdominal muscles. A quick release and contract accent is known as a "belly pop."

Glute contraction: A contraction of the gluteus muscles isolated to one buttock at a time. Popularized in American belly dance by Suhaila Salimpour, glute contractions along with core control, strengthen and sharpen hip movements.

Hip Twist: A horizontal twist performed by contracting or stretching the oblique muscles.

Hip Slide: A horizontal lateral hip stretch initiated from the obliques. Lengthen the back muscles and shift center of gravity for a hip slide from front to back.

Pelvic Drop: A downward movement of the pelvis releasing the lower abdominal muscles and contracting the lower back muscles.

Pelvic Lift (tuck): The opposite of a pelvic drop, executed by releasing or stretching the lower back muscles and contracting the lower abdominal muscles.

Hip Tilt: A tilt of the pelvis, stretching the obliques on one side while contracting on the other, to tilt one hip lower than the other, like a see-saw.

Articulations and Movements

Horizontal Hip Figure 8: hip slide + hip twist. This move is actually the shape of the infinity sign on the floor ∞, which the hips trace. Direction can be inward (back to front) or outward (front to back).

Vertical Hip Figure 8 up (inward): hip slide + hip tilt up. This movement is also an infinity sign. Imagine tracing this pattern on the wall or mirror with the front of your hips, or on the wall behind you with your buttocks.

Vertical Hip Figure 8 down (outward): hip slide + hip tilt down. Also known as *maya*. This is the opposite of the vertical hip figure 8 up or inward.

Hip Lift: hip tilt upward on non-weighted standing position initiated by contracting obliques with heel off the floor. Variations include hip twist. The accent is on the upward motion.

Hip Drop: Movement starts with hip lift position. The drop is a controlled release through the abs and obliques and can be aided by a gluteus contraction on the opposite (weighted) side to create a percussive movement. The accent is on the downward motion.

Pelvic Circle: This is a dynamic three-dimensional move also referred to as *omi* or *umi* and has two variations. Start with pelvis tucked in and up. Then hip tilt down on R + pelvic drop (release)/hip tilt down on L + pelvic/hip tilt lift R + pelvic/hip lift L. This variation emphasizes the downward motion of the circle (pelvis releases down on the down beat of the music). The other variation starts with pelvis released, then hip tilt up R+ pelvic lift/hip tilt up L + hip tilt down R + pelvic drop/hip tilt down L, emphasizes the lift or upward motion of the circle (pelvis pulls up on the down beat of the music). The direction of this move may also be described as clockwise or counter clockwise, though that may be more difficult to visualize since it is not a flat movement.

Hip Circle: Abdominal contraction + hip slide side + hip slide back + hip slide to other side + shift to center/neutral. The knees remain soft, however the pelvis does not tilt as in the pelvic circle. The size of the circle is proportional to how far apart the feet are -- the wider the stance, the potential for a larger movement.

Hip Sway: Glute contraction + hip tilt + hip slide or shift of weight side to side.

Hip Shimmy: Fast, alternating hip tilt controlled through the obliques.

Leg Shimmy: Fast, gentle alternating bending and straightening of the knees. This is a loose jiggle of the thighs and buttocks while engaging the core without tilting the hips. The knees should never lock in the straightened position during this movement.

Upper Body

Upper body movements, specifically, ribcage isolations, in the context of this curriculum guide, are primarily used as exercises to develop skills rather than essential movements. Chest isolations condition the postural muscles and help with developing confidence and grace in arm movements. Ribcage articulations, particularly figure 8's (infinity patterns), help to develop fluidity required in turns, transitions and directional changes. Furthermore, these exercises develop core flexibility that helps a dancer gain full control of her body for dynamic musicality and freedom of self-expression.

Isolations

Ribcage slide (chest slide): A horizontal shift of the ribcage side-to-side or forward and back, engaging the obliques, upper abdominal, and pectoral muscles.

Ribcage lift (chest lift): A lift of the ribcage using the upper abdominal muscle on the down beat.

Ribcage drop (chest drop): A downward accent of the ribcage using the upper abdominal and upper back muscles beginning with a soft lift, followed by a controlled release on the down beat.

Ribcage twist: A rotation of the ribcage using the obliques and latissimus muscles in the upper back, which brings one shoulder forward while the other back.

Ribcage tilt: Engaging the obliques to lift and tilt the ribcage, bringing one shoulder higher than the other, like a see-saw.

Shoulder Accent: A sharp movement performed with the pectoral muscles and the trapezius muscles in the upper back. The accent may push the shoulder forward, back or up.

Articulations and Movements

Horizontal Ribcage Circle: Ribcage slide fwd + ribcage slide to the side, drawing a circle on the floor with the sternum. The movement can be drawn clockwise or counter clockwise.

Vertical Ribcage Circle: Ribcage slide to the side + ribcage lift, drawing a circle on the wall or mirror with the sternum. The movement can be drawn clockwise or counter clockwise.

Horizontal Ribcage Figure 8: Ribcage side + ribcage twist, his movement is a figure of eight (infinity pattern) on the floor with the sternum. The direction of this movement can be back to front (inward) or front to back (outward).

Vertical Ribcage Figure 8: Ribcage lift + ribcage slide, a figure of eight movement (infinity pattern) drawing the infinity sign on the wall or mirror. The direction of this movement can be down to up (inward), or up to down (outward).

Shoulder Roll: A soft rotation of the shoulder forward, up, back and down; or back, up, forward and down using the pectoral and trapezius muscles.

Shoulder Shimmy: Shoulder accents in rapid succession and may also include small twisting motion of the ribcage.

Snake arms: Shoulder roll from the trapezius muscles and pectorals combined with gentle lift and relax of the elbows, alternating right to left. Ribcage twist, slide or figure 8 adds additional layers and texture this movement.

Upper body undulation: Another type of vertical ribcage circle where the sternum draws the circle forward, up, back and down to neutral, ie. chest slide forward + chest lift+ chest slide back + chest drop or release (relax).

Full body undulation: The upper body undulation followed by a lower body undulation in which both movements are performed sequentially. As the upper undulation is about to be completed, the lower body undulation begins.

Steps, Pivots and Turns

All of our steps can be varied with pivots, level changes, floor patterns, and body movements. When one part of the step is changed, or an element of movement with the body or arms is added, the step can take on new life to suite the mood, flavor, and style of music, as well as the dancer's preference.

Steps

Step-Touch: Step with the right foot, then touch with the left foot. Repeat, step with left, touch with the right. The count is: 1 step, 2 touch.

Cross-Point: A variation of step-touch, cross and step the right foot over left, then point or touch with the left foot.

Step-Pivot: Similar to the basic step-touch, this step uses a pivot on the standing foot to change direction. This dynamic can be combined with the basic step-touch and the cross-point to make variations on the weight shift pattern. Step right foot forward, touch and propel with the left to pivot on the ball of the right foot. Pivot direction can be open (outward) or closed (inward).

Step-Close-Step: Also known as the shuffle step or side-step. Take a step to the side with the right foot, close and step with the left. A typical combination is: 1 step, 2 close, 3 step, 4 close and touch. However, the step may be repeated to suit the music or level of students.

Two-Step: Feet are in fourth position. Keep the position of the feet while stepping. There three main variations of this step. The differences are primarily in the timing tempo of the step.

Variations:

> **Rock Step (half time):** Step R foot forward, L foot back, holding each step for an addition count: 1 step forward, 2 hold/rock, 3 step L back, 4 hold/rock
>
> **Flat-Ball (full time):** Step right foot flat, step left on the ball, step right on the ball, step left on the ball, ie. flat, ball, ball, ball or fwd flat, back ball, fwd ball, back ball. In full time, the count: 1 step R, 2 step L. In double time, the count time: 1 step R, AND step L, 2 step R, AND step L.

Tip-Toe (double/quadruple time): Keep the feet very close together, the body very tall and lifted and all the muscles in the thighs thoroughly engaged with soft knees, make small quick steps laterally, keeping the feet very close together, with the lead foot slightly forward. The double-time step count is: 1 step R, AND step L, 2 step R, AND step L, 3 step R, AND step L, 4 step 4, AND step L (1AND2AND3AND4AND). The quadruple-time step count is: 1 step R, e step L, AND step R, a step L, 2 step R, e step L, And step R, a step L (1eANDa2eANDa3eANDa4eANDa).

Three-Step: *step-ball-change, cha-cha-cha,* or *chassé*. Step right, quick step left, step right. Three steps that fit to two beats of music. RLR, LRL. The count is: 1 step R, AND step L, 2 step R.

Four-Step: *scissor step, sharqi step, box step*. This is a 4/4 step with the lead foot stepping forward and back. The count is: 1 step R fwd, 2 step L in place, 3 step R back, 4 step L in place. This step can also be performed in double time.

Grapevine: Cross and step the right foot over the left, step to the side with the left, cross and step the right foot behind the left, step to the side with the left, ie. cross front, step side, cross back, step side. Repeat to R with Left leading. The count is: 1 cross R over L, 2 step L side, 3 cross R back, 4 step L side. Variations include starting the step with any of the three foot positions, ie. stepping to the side, crossing front, or crossing back.

Pivots and Turns

A pivot for every weight change will create different types of turns. Pivots and turns may be open or closed. An open turn is away from the center of the body. A closed turn is toward the center of the body.

Pivot: a change of direction.

2-step Turn: A pivot on each weight change of a two-step combination.

3-step Turn: A pivot on each weight change of a three-step combination.

3

Music Fundamentals

As a belly dance instructor, it is essential that you understand the fundamentals of Middle Eastern music, rhythms and instruments. Without this essential knowledge, many parts of this curriculum will be difficult to follow and teach. If you need supplemental education in this area, look for workshops, DVD's and online resources to help you form a solid understanding of the music and how it relates to the dance.

10 Essential Rhythms

1. Maqsoum

Basic rhythm with many varieties, tempos and modes, with a bouncy and steady four-beat structure good for all basic hip movements, back or downward movements, and basic steps. This is the foundation rhythm of the most commonly used rhythms in Oriental dance music.

D T   T D   T

1 A 2 A 3 A 4

2. Masmoudi Saghir ("Baladi")

Same structure as Maqsoum, but the first two accented beats are DD rather than DT. At slow to medium tempos, the accented beats are good for quick successive isolations and accents, as well as steps and combinations. The correct name for this rhythm is masmoudi saghir, however many American dancers and drummers refer to this rhythm as baladi.

D D   T D   T

1 A 2 A 3 A 4

3. Saidi

Egyptian folkloric rhythm and dance styles, which include the characteristic hopping steps and bouncy movements. A four-beat structure similar to *baladi* but with the accented beats reversed, this rhythm is good for rhythmic accents, stepping patterns and playful combinations.

D T   DD   T

1 A 2 A3 A 4

4. Fellahi

The name refers to the *Felaheen* or Egyptian farmers. Very fast version of Maqsoum made to fit a two-beat structure. This upbeat Egyptian folkloric rhythm and dance style has a characteristic step, hops and fast articulated hip shimmies with traveling.

DTDT

1A2A

5. Ayoub

Associated with trance and healing rituals, it has a very heavy but simple two-beat structure and is good for isolations, upward or forward movements, and two-step patterns.

D DT

1A2A

6. Malfuf

A folkloric rhythm that has a rolling sound suitable for many varieties of three-step and two-step combinations. The characteristic step associated with this rhythm is the three-step chassé, which is used often in Oriental styling to travel the stage.

D TT

1 A2

7. Chiftitelli/Wahda Kabira/Wahda Sonbati

An eight-beat rhythm great for slow and circular movements, figure 8s, patterns and lyrical combinations. Often heard in the musical form, *Taqasim*.

D TTD   T
12**34**5**6**7**8**

8. Wahda

Similar feel to chiftitelli, wahda is a four-beat rhythm widely used in Egyptian music, great for slow and circular movements. Often heard in the musical form, *Taqasim*. Notice the structure is the same as malfuf, stretched over four beats instead of two.

D   T T
1 2 **3 4**

9. Masmoudi Kabir

An eight-beat rhythm associated with classical Egyptian Oriental music as well the Arabo-Andalusi style of dance and music. This rhythm lends itself well to interpretation of a wide range of horizontal skill-building lessons. Notice the structure is similar to masmoudi saghir (little masmoudi), stretched over eight beats instead of four.

D D   T D T   T
1 2 3 4 **5 6** 7 **8**

10. 3/4 or Walz

With the same structure and feel as the western version, this rhythm has a smooth rolling feel making it an easy rhythm to practice three-step combinations, turns and other dynamic movements.

D T T
1 2 3

Melodic Instruments

As with popular rhythms, melodic instruments can be associated with specific movements. While there are no set rules, assigning characteristics to the sounds of instruments can help students capture the feeling of the movement with their bodies and learn more about the music.

- *Nay* – upper body, Veil (wind, spiritual)

- *Oud* – arms, shoulders (rain, mystical)

- *Accordion* – undulations, circles, figure eights, stretchy hip and upper body movements (waves, mischievous)

- *Violin* – undulations, circles, figure eights, stretchy hip and upper body movements (crying, storytelling)

- *Brass / saxophone, trumpet* – vertical movements (fire, sassy or playful, romantic)

- *Khanoun* – vibrating shimmies (earthy or intellectual)

The rhythm establishes the pattern of movements and steps, and can help identify the cultural flavor of the music. When selecting movement vocabulary for a specific piece of music, the melody is actually the main attraction of the piece. The underlying rhythm is a great foundation for portraying the origin and purpose of the piece. However, it is the melody that tells the story. The melody draws us in and evokes our emotions.

The human voice is also considered a melodic instrument. Syllables and intonation in the language and the meaning of the lyrics are all essential elements. You should at least know the general idea of the songs you use in class and performances, especially for a specific or ethnically mixed audience.

Selecting Music for Class

Music selections should propel the movements and engage the students. The music moves the class forward toward its exciting culmination and inspires feelings of tranquility at the end. From the warm-up to combinations and dance style, the music should connect the concepts and skills you are teaching.

Select music that serves the purpose of the instruction and is pleasant. Some criteria to listen for in drills and practice music include:

- A steady beat or easy to hear rhythmic patterns

- Phrasing in clearly audible 8 count measures

- Length of the song is appropriate for the specific drill or learning goal

- Specific rhythms or styles that connect to the learning goal or routine

The music can serve as a memory trigger for you, and can help students recall movements and combinations typically performed to a specific rhythm or song. Incorporating a variety of traditional music and rhythms offers a great opportunity to learn more about the various cultural styles associated with belly dance, and to share that knowledge with your students.

When using music with lyrics, even instrumental versions, it is a good idea to know the meaning of the song. Students are often curious and will ask what the song is saying. When this happens, you should have a general idea of what the lyrics mean. Ex. "His lady left him and he's begging the world to help him find her."

This curiosity should be nurtured and encouraged every chance you get. You may be amazed how it will enhance your class experience and give you added credibility as a highly qualified instructor.

Compiling Playlists

Create a variety of playlists for your purposes. Time your playlist to provide ample opportunity for practice and repetition. At the same time be sure students are engaged in a variety of movements that allow them to exercise all the different muscle groups during each class.

Use the principles of **Repetition & Routine**, **Variety** and **Culmination**, to inspire music selection and class structure.

Repetition & Routine

Some aspects of your class should rarely change. It is important to establish a standard routine that students can predict. Make it purposeful and positive because it will develop into a habit. Along with routine, music selection should offer ample opportunity for repetition of specific movements and combinations throughout the duration of the class.

Variety

Some parts of your class should change more frequently. Even one small change can make a difference. There are many ways to add variety, including changing the order of the music, adding one or two new songs, adding embellishments to basic moves, or exploring a new style or technique for a familiar step or move. In addition, you can work on a familiar combination and bring attention to the musicality or cultural context; share a personal experience, and/or ask students to share their perspective on a familiar move or combination as they practice.

Culmination

Each class should culminate in some kind of activity that ties many or all of the concepts together. This is typically a choreographed sequence or drill routine; even a very basic choreography can instill confidence and a sense of achievement; it can also be a follow-me drill that you create on the spot or a loosely choreographed routine.

4
Layering & Build-Up Method

The layering and build-up method is the hallmark of this format. I was introduced to the idea through the instructional videos of Mohammad Khordadian, the famous Iranian dancer and fitness instructor. His aerobics-style Persian dance videos demonstrated the layering of body articulations on top of foot positions, pivots and simple weight changes, to create dynamic movement combinations. I began to apply this concept in my personal belly dance practice. It worked brilliantly with infinite variations and combinations of movements, steps and dynamics.

Not long after, I created a homemade card game based on this method. I wrote the names of movements, steps and dance elements on pieces of paper and randomly selected cards to combine. The combined cards created interesting movement combinations. I called it "The Layering Game." Years later, I have created an official game, graduating from little pieces of paper to actual playing cards. I still play when I feel like challenging my students or myself.

When you learn this layering method, you will no longer struggle to break down movements. Incidentally, I do not want you to ever break down another movement again. Ever. Here's why. To break something down means to destroy it. Why not build it up instead? Building up the movement from its foundation creates stronger technique and is easier to understand.

The layering and build up method uses the movement vocabulary, ie. the language of the dance, to define and describe the dynamics of dance movement. In this format, we create combinations from the very basic components, and add one element at a time to describe what is happening in the body and how it is interacting with the space it occupies.

The layering and build-up method is based on the simple idea that dance movement is easier to learn when it is built up, rather than broken down. Even complex combinations can articulated with this method.

The method is sequential and follows a logical order that is natural for the body to incorporate:

1. Begin simply with a foot position or pose.
2. Next, add any isolation or movement.
3. Then a weight shift. Movements can be accented over the weighted or unweighted foot.
4. Listen for cues in the music and add more movements or isolations.
5. Dynamic traveling can now occur.
6. Travelling in a floor pattern is now possible, while performing all of the elements simultaneously.

I. Step & Movement Combinations

A. Step-Touch

1. **Step-Touch** front, side or back, or **Cross-Touch**. Same concept, different foot positions.

2. Add to or replace **Touch** with:
   - Abdominal contract or release (belly pop)
   - Hip lift
   - Hip twist
   - Hip lift and drop
   - Knee lift
   - Hop or heel pulse

3. Layer onto **Step**:
   - Vertical or horizontal figure 8 (each step gets half of the ∞)
   - Hip twist (this looks like a fwd-back shimmy, or what is sometimes called "the washing machine")

4. Travel and/or change directions

5. Replace **Touch** with a pivot turn (**Step-Pivot**)

B. Step-Close-Step (expand Step-Touch)
1. All options from basic Step-Touch
2. Break up each repetition with any standing movement

C. Three-Step (Chassé)
Add to each step
- Glute contractions (half-time 3/4 shimmy)
- Leg shimmy
- Hip circle
- Undulation

D. Four-Step
1. Add to each step:
   - Shoulder shimmy
   - 3/4 hip shimmy
2. Add to the first step only:
   - Chest lift and shoulder shimmy
   - Hip twist
   - A hop
3. Add to back step:
   - Knee lift
   - Hip slide (to the side or to the back)
4. Pause at end of measure to change lead foot
5. Add travel and direction changes, ie. floor pattern

E. Grapevine
1. Cross front only or cross back only (this might be consider a two-step variation)
2. Add hip tilt on front cross
3. Add shoulder shimmy or arm paths and patterns

F. Two-Step variations

1. Add to forward step only:
   - Abdominal release
   - Hip twist
   - Glute contraction
   - Undulation (starts on front foot, release on back foot, emphasis on inward movement, ie. abdominal contraction)
   - Horizontal hip circle (starts on front foot with hip slide, then the hip circles inward)

2. Level and timing variations
   - Flat-ball, ball-flat
   - Rock-step (half-time)
   - Tip-toe (double time)

3. Add upper body movements:
   - Chest lift or drop (or both: chest lift on front step; chest drop on back step)

II. Pivots, Turns and Spins - Add onto or combine with basic steps

1. One-step pivot
2. Two-step turn
3. Three-step turn
4. Spin steps or continuous turns in 4, 8 or 16 count phrases

III. Arms, Hands and Expression - Add to pivots and turn

1. Arm circles and figure 8s'
2. Arm sweeps and wrist circles
3. Follow the move with a visual focus, carry momentum through with gentle head circle or figure 8

IV. Rhythms

A. *Explore Rhythms* – Find the "Doums"

1. Maqsoum – Medium tempo, with all variations of steps and movements.
2. Baladi – Slower tempo, find soft and sharp accents on the "Doum" along with fluid movements for the rest.
3. Saidi – Folkloric styling with loose, bouncy movements as well as subtle variations.
4. Fellahi – Fast tempo, with step variations for traveling half time or full time.
5. Ayoub – Slow and fast tempos with circular movements.
6. Chiftitelli/Sonbati – slow and medium tempos with fluid body movements as well as accents and isolations.
7. Malfuf – fast tempo with quick traveling steps and floor patterns.
8. Wahda – slow and medium tempo with undulations and slow step variations.
9. Masmoudi – Slow and medium tempos, find soft and sharp accents on "Doum", then fluid movements and turns.
10. Waltz – Medium to fast tempos, with three-step traveling, floor patterns and turns.

B. *Listen for Texture, Phrasing and Meaning*

1. Maintain the structure and style of music with the base rhythm through footwork and stepping patterns.
2. Embellish secondary percussion sounds with lower body movements.
3. Capture the flavor of the main melodic instrument(s), orchestra or lyrics with upper body movements.
4. Interact subtly through head and facial expressions with secondary melodic instrument(s). Often this is a call-and-response between the melodic instruments and the orchestra.
5. Tell the story. Research the song if needed, then explore and express yourself freely.

5

Class Structure, Sequence & Pace

Sessions are presented in six-week plans. There are two six-week plans for each thematic unit. Each six-week plan may be taught as a stand-alone session or you may combine session plans in whole or in part to create longer sessions. For example, if your class sessions are eight weeks long, you can combine a six-week session plan with two individual lessons from another six-week plan to fill your eight-week session.

Session plans can be progressive so that continuing students will build on their skills and knowledge from one session to the next. However, when you present each session, assume no prior knowledge. No matter the experience or level of students, each session must begin with the same foundational concepts.

Thematic Units

Fall: Foundations in Folklore

Students explore the foundations of belly dance through its folkloric roots. Dance movements will be presented in the context of rhythms and musical forms associated with folkloric styles such as baladi, saidi and fellahi.

Winter: Music & Choreography

Students explore belly dance with a focus on musicality and choreography. At the beginner level, these concepts are presented very simply and will be revisited often as students progress throughout the program.

Spring: Performance Skills

Students explore belly dance as a performance art. At this level, performance skills teach poise and confidence. Activities and exercises focus on enriching and advancing the individual, not necessarily preparing a performance for an audience. Though, that could be an option.

Summer: Specialty & Review Topics

Students explore and review elements of dance and performance styles that enrich and enhance their experience. Specialty topics may include props such as Veil Dancing, or musical forms such as Drum Solo. Review topics may include specific techniques selected from the various seasonal themes, such as Shimmies, Figure Eights and Undulations.

Class Structure

While each teacher will bring his or her unique strengths and interests to the dance classroom, there are some key components that contribute to a successful and enjoyable experience. Practice these three key elements of a fun and productive session:

- **Stay organized.** Use this manual and practice your delivery and sequence of material. Don't panic if you get a little mixed up while teaching. It happens. Just go with it or move on to something else. You will get better with experience.

- **Establish a routine and structure from the very first class.** Don't experiment with different formats in the same session. Maintain a structure and routine students can predict, while continually adding new things.

- **Keep the pace moving.** A good class structure steadily progresses in a logical sequence of activities that culminate in the learning objectives. A thoughtfully compiled playlist can help you remember the sequence of activities and engage the students.

An effective class structure is enjoyable and has a progressive sequence, but is also flexible when you need it. When structuring your class, you will need to make adjustments along the way that consider the level of your students, your teaching style, type of class, as well as learning objectives.

Time management can be one of biggest challenges for teachers. New and experienced teachers alike can struggle with staying on track. We have so much to share and we are extremely patient with our students, both of which are good! However, getting sidetracked and distracted too often, can lead to losing your train of thought and eventually to chaos.

Stay on task and keep the pace of the class moving along. Don't over-do a move, especially if some students are still struggling. Move on and revisit the concept in a future class. Keep discussion and lecture simple, adhering to a strict five-minute limit. Discussions should be relevant to the topic and level of students. It is best to move on from sticky topics and address them another time in manageable parts that are appropriate for the students' interests and level of experience. If a topic is of great interest but getting out of control, you can refocus the class by saying something like,

> *"Those are all really good points, and I would love for us to explore them. Let me look into it/think about it, and perhaps we can have an online discussion/find a website/have a workshop, to delve deeper into this topic/figure it out. In the meantime, let's continue with the lesson."*

As the teacher, it is your job to keep everyone on task and move the class forward. Throughout this manual, we will format lesson plans based on a 50 to 60 minute class with the following sequence and structure:

1. **Welcome, Introduction and Warm-Up (10-12 minutes)**
2. **Stationary Isolations and Movements (10-12 minutes)**
3. **Practice Activity: Movement Combinations or Steps (15-18 minutes)**
4. **Culminating activity: Choreography or Drill Sequence (5-7 minutes)**
5. **Final Activity: Follow the Teacher or Shimmy Drill (2-4 minutes)**
6. **Cool down, Stretching and Relaxation (5-8 minutes)**
7. **Gratitude and Final Remarks or Reminders**

Each section will correspond to the tracks on your class playlist. In the next section, we'll explore each part of the class and its progression from beginning to end.

Class Sequence

1. Introduction & Warm-up

Welcome your students! Tell them the general objectives of the class and what they can expect. Ask if there are any injuries and make a note to watch those individuals more closely. Tell everyone to listen to their bodies and take it easy or stop if they feel any pain.

Take one or two minutes at the most, to bring awareness to general stance, and give a tip that will help students feel less pressure and more successful as you move through the warm up.

> **Example:** *"Let's take a moment to bring awareness to our feet and feel how your body shifts weight as you step in place. We'll learn more about stance and body alignment in a few minutes. For now, I just need you to feel your feet and the pull of gravity as you shift your body weight. Good. We're going to start with a gentle warm-up.*
>
> *Try to relax and move along with me. Don't worry if your moves are not exactly like mine. Observe and follow the feet and weight changes first. That will help you put the hips in the right place when the time comes. By the end of class tonight, you will all be moving together in perfect time to the music. Let's get started!"*

This may seem extremely elementary for some students. For others, it may be essential for them to feel successful, or at least comfortable, knowing it is not prerequisite knowledge.

Refrain from too much talking in the beginning of class unless it is necessary for the safety of students. New students may be nervous and definitely excited to get started. So get started and get moving!

> **a. Fast warm-up:** Choose a medium tempo song with a simple structure and rich sound. The fast warm up should be very basic and gentle.
>
> **Example:** Begin by swaying and shifting weight from side to side at half time for 8 – 16 counts. Speed up to full time and merge weight shifts with a simple Step-Touch pattern, adding body movements one at a time to the same repetitive stepping pattern:
>
> - Step-touch-reach side to side
> - Step-touch shoulder roll
> - Step-touch-extend foot (tap toe)

- Step-hip twist
- Step-hip walk forward
- Step-touch walk back
- Step-lift knee (to 90 degree angle)
- Step-cross-lean

b. Slow warm-up: Choose a slow tempo song with a simple structure and a rich sound.

Example: Begin with a series of cat and dog yoga stretches in a crouched straddle stance from a flat back to round back, focus on engaging the lower abdominals. Repeat about eight times. Next, perform the exercise in a standing position, focus on engaging the upper abdominals, rounding the back and shoulders, then extend and stretch to open the chest and arms. Repeat about 8 times. Continue the slow warm-up with large circular movements of the torso, arms and legs. Include ankle circles in both directions. Finish the slow warm-up with gentle neck stretches.

c. Warm-up Isolations: Choose a fun up-tempo song with a distinct beat and a repetitive structure.

Example: Start in standing position in normal stance for lower body core awareness exercises. Then instruct students to stand in a straddle semi-squat position (slight plié in second position, i.e. wide stance) and firmly anchor the feet, legs and hips. You will take the time more in-depth after this exercise to address dance posture and body alignment. For now, get students moving. Begin with core muscle engagement, starting with abdominal isolations and move up to chest isolations. Face the students when demonstrating these muscle engagement exercises, and then move around to show the movements from different angles.

Standing position:

- Abdominal contract and release (no pelvic movement)
- Hip slide (knees soft, weight centered)

Straddle semi-squat (Wide stance plié):
- Chest lift
- Chest slide
- Chest twist
- Shoulder accents

d. Body Awareness, Alignment & Muscle Engagement: Choose a slow tempo song with a soft flowing melody or gentle repetitive rhythm. Take a few minutes to bring awareness to the different joints and body parts and how to get into the proper alignment and posture for the stationary exercises.

> **Feet:** Hip-width apart (hip-bone apart)
>
> **Center of Gravity:** Weight evenly distributed over the front of the feet
>
> **Knees:** Soft and relaxed
>
> **Pelvis:** Gently tucked to neutral position and aligned with the spine
>
> **Ribcage:** Lifted and slightly forward
>
> **Shoulders:** Relaxed and down
>
> **Head:** Long neck and chin level
>
> **Arms:** Extended with soft elbows lifted just below shoulder level

2. Stationary Exercises: Review & Practice of Movements

Begin with abdominal awareness and control. You may wish to have students sit on the floor in order to better locate and engage the specific muscle groups. Remember to face the students first, then demonstrate from different angles.

Introduce or review a variety of basic body isolations that are the building blocks of the movements and concepts that you will be teaching in the day's lesson. Observe students, and guide them in maintaining proper alignment and muscle engagement.

Example. Lesson plan incorporates hip figure 8's and snake arms.

> **Lower Body Isolations for Hip Figure 8's**
> - Abdominal contract and release
> - Hip slide side-to-side
> - Glute contract and release
> - Hip tilt
> - Hip slide fwd-back
> - Hip twist
>
> **Upper Body Isolations for Snake Arms**
> - Chest lift
> - Ribcage twist
> - Trapezius isolations, merge with shoulder accent forward

In this section, you may also wish to review a combination or concept from a previous lesson.

3. Introduce & Practice New Movements, Steps & Combinations

This section should be the highlight of an hour-long class. Choose two to three songs with a medium-slow tempo with a generic beat or steady rhythm that correspond to the music, culture and artistry, and learning objectives of the day's lesson. Engage students in dynamic movement. The purpose of this section is to practice putting together the learning objectives of the lesson plan. There can be a great amount of variety in this section from week to week. When you're ready to add new material and music, this is the place to focus on bringing all of your creative ideas, even the crazy ones. This is the time to really challenge students or help them improve beyond the previous week. Keep the pace moving and have fun with it!

> **Example.** Practice a 16-count combination of movements or across the floor exercise of basic steps. Practice movements and combinations in 16, 8 and 4 count phrases. Throughout the exercise, remind students about muscle engagement and alignment. Demonstrate the movement or combination at half time, then speed up to full time.

4. Culminating Activity - Combination, Choreography or Drill Sequence

Before beginning the culminating activity, ask if there are any questions. Challenge students to put some or all of the skills together as you cue them to follow along. Before you begin, make sure to ask if there are any questions about what you have covered. You may want to add a short slow or quiet song into your playlist just before so that you have time to answer questions or go over a few reminders before you jump into the routine or activity. If the routine is a piece you are working on over the course of the session, but have only covered a portion of it, let students know that they will learn the rest later and that it is OK if they stumble along through the parts that have not yet been covered.

5. Final Activity - Follow the Teacher or Shimmy Drill (Optional)

End the class with a short, fun, and very simple activity that will be accessible to all students, such as a very basic improvised sequence, a.k.a. "Follow-the-Bouncing-Butt," or a simple shimmy drill. These short simplified activities can help develop interest in future topics and lay the foundation for future skill building of complex concepts.

6. Cool-down & Stretch

Bring the energy level down, especially if the class is high energy. Bring the heart rate down slowly, then transition to stretching sequences for the torso, legs and upper body. You can take this time to end with meditative movements and encourage breathing and body awareness, and to promote a sense of peace and relaxation. At this point in the class experience, it is completely up to you what message you want to communicate to your students.

7. Gratitude

Take 10 seconds to thank your students for coming to your class and for the opportunity to share dance with them. Congratulate them on a job well done. You can also give them something to look forward to by telling them a little bit about the next class.

◊ ◊ ◊

Individual sections of this class structure may be expanded or condensed based upon the needs of the students or time considerations. However, unless you have a compelling reason, do not spend too much time on any one thing.

The key to a fun class is to maintain a routine and keep the pace while adding one or two new things in every class. If you practice teaching with this formula, your students will look forward to coming to class and you will become a more confident and experienced instructor.

After each class, reflect on the lesson and experience. Evaluate what went well and be proud of it. Use it to develop your strengths. Reflect on what could have been better and what you would do differently next time. You may also enjoy keeping a teacher's journal to record your thoughts and ideas. You may feel the most insightful and inspired right after class, when your brain is active and engaged, and your body is full of endorphins.

Course Pace and Progression

Progression of class content follows a sequence that builds on skills from week to week in the context of the unit's theme. Review of the previous week's material is implicit when following the session plan from beginning to end.

The table on the next page maps the course progression of a twelve-week unit, which may be taught in two six-week sessions, if desired. Notice that the first and second half of the unit mirror in content, with a slightly different focus in each half. This is more apparent in the actual lesson plans from week to week when you review the thematic units.

Twelve-Week Unit Progression

Part 1

Week #	Technique	Music & Culture	Artistry
1	Isolations	Timing & Phrasing	Pose and Stance
2	Horizontal Movements	Characteristic rhythm or instrument	Body Lines
3	Vertical Movements	Characteristic rhythm or instrument	Fluidity
4	Steps/Traveling	Rhythm & Melody	Pattern and Direction
5	Traveling/Dynamic Combination	Characteristic song	Interpretation
6	Choreography or Drill Routine	Musicality/Context	Flavor and Expression

Part 2

Week #	Technique	Music & Culture	Artistry
1 or 7	Isolations	Timing & Phrasing	Pose and Stance
2 or 8	Shimmies	Characteristic rhythm	Body Lines
3 or 9	Upper Body/Arms, Pivots/Turns	Characteristic rhythm	Fluidity
4 or 10	Steps/Traveling	Rhythm & Melody	Pattern and Direction
5 or 11	Traveling/Dynamic Combination	Characteristic song	Interpretation
6 or 12	Choreography or Drill Routine	Musicality/Context	Flavor and Expression

You may wish to modify the order of progression based on the session theme or choreography requirements. For example, if shimmies appear in the beginning of your choreography or are an integral part of your choreography, you may wish to move the shimmies class to part 1, and start working on shimmies in the second or third week of the session.

Grading rubrics for student evaluation purposes are included for each unit. I do not believe in grading students formally in a recreational setting, unless asked by the student. Usually, the students' personal growth and progress is evidenced in their enhanced quality of life. However, when it is necessary to determine and document whether a student has achieved the learning goals, grading rubrics can be a very useful tool.

Grading Rubrics for Student Evaluation (optional)

Objectives	Needs reinforcement	Solid understanding, benefits from practice	Mastery, enjoys advanced exploration
1			
2			
3			
4			
5			
6			
7			
8			
9			
10			

Teaching Strategies for Drop-in and Multilevel Classes

As you build on each component and begin practicing a movement or combination, demonstrate the most basic version of the movement or combination first for lower level students. For those ready for a challenge, or ready for the next layer, demonstrate the advanced version.

There are three components to creating a successful multilevel program:

1. *A thematic approach with topics relevant to all levels*

Choose a theme for each class.

Use the unit themes to inspire lesson themes for each individual class. This is somewhat done in the weekly plans, but you may wish to further highlight or modify these themes based on your own ideas and music choices.

2. *An organized, progressive and flexible class structure*

Keep the pace moving toward a desired goal.

Progress the class forward with defined objective. Begin with the end in mind and stay on task toward this goal.

3. *A common foundational springboard for all levels*

Start every class with the basics.

Every class should begin with the principals of body alignment and muscle engagement, adding to and progressing the previous concept. Again, master the movement vocabulary and use the layering & build-up method. Here is the sequence for adding the different dance components:

    1. Beginner/Easy - Steps and feet

    2. Advanced Beginner - Hips/body movements

    3. Advanced Beginner - Posture and arms

    4. Intermediate/Advanced – Turns, pivots, accents and nuances

Other strategies include:

- Offer timing and tempo options, such as quarter time and half time. Keep in mind some movements are actually easier to perform at a medium tempo rather than slow tempo, so practice at different tempos.

- Instruct more experienced dancers to explore the advanced version without instructor lead, while you continue to lead the rest of the class in the basic version. The main reason for this is simple: it is natural to mimic the teacher. Less experienced students will always try to mimic the teacher. They may feel awkward not doing the full robust or advanced version that you and others are doing. Another reason is that less experienced students may be eager to put it all together, even when they need to spend more time with the basic version.

- Whenever possible, encourage experienced students to explore the advanced version of the concepts you are teaching. If they are ready for the advanced concepts, they should perform that version of the movement or combination on their own. If they don't, discretely encourage them individually to try the advanced version. Be sure to revert everyone back to the basic version if they begin to get flustered, fatigued or lose proper form. You may also choose to toggle between the basic and advanced version.

Successfully teaching multiple levels of students simultaneously requires much practice. It also requires that you trust the process and principals of the layering and build-up method. Have faith in yourself and commit to practicing these multilevel teaching strategies until they become part of your teaching style. You will grow more confident with experience.

Feedback & Correction

Feedback and correction from the instructor is an important part of learning. It also establishes rapport with students. Most students want to learn the right way to do what you ask and appreciate it when you take the time to notice their efforts. Whether you offer correction to some and praise to others, remember, people always remember how you made them feel and not necessarily what was said or done.

When offering feedback, be sure to consider whether the student has any injuries or other issues. If so, make it a point to learn how you can adjust your instruction for them, by either asking the student for more information or doing your own research.

Correcting mistakes is primarily rooted in correcting alignment and muscle engagement. The primary culprit in most alignment mistakes is not engaging the core muscles. In addition, look for alignment issues in the shoulders, elbows, lower back, knees, and feet.

Common alignment mistakes in performing upper body movements:
- Closed or droopy chest → not engaging upper back and abdominal muscles
- Elbows rotated up, shoulders hunched forward → not engaging pectorals
- Bent elbows → not engaging upper back and pectorals

Common alignment mistakes in performing lower body movements:
- Arched lower back → not engaging core muscles
- Stiff hip movements → locking the knees
- Jerky movements → not engaging the abs or glutes

There are many ways to help students become aware of their bodies and achieve precise beautiful movements. Imagery and analogies are fun and inspiring. Students also appreciate knowing where they should feel the movements on their bodies. Whether you use the correct anatomical names or not, show on your body where the movement initiates. Ask students to feel their own muscles and joints at work.

Tips for Offering Feedback and Correction:
- Show students how to self-correct by demonstrating 'what not to do' and stating clearly what you do NOT want to see along with what you DO want to see. Ask students to observe in the mirror the mechanics of their own form and alignment. Show them how to use muscle engagement to correct the position of the spine and other joints.
- To avoid singling out students, make eye contact with specific students without making it obvious to whom you are referring
- Walk around and give individual corrections to students in a low tone, followed by a loud enthusiastic praise when the correction is made
- Note something that all or most students are doing right or that you enjoy seeing

Common Alignment Mistakes

Part II

Thematic Units & Lesson Plans

Introduction

Begin with the End in Mind

When preparing your session, begin with the end in mind. Work backward from the session objectives to create combinations or choreography that impart the concepts of the unit's theme. You may also begin with specific choreography as a goal, and draw your objectives from the themes and concepts of the choreography.

You will have teaching objectives for each lesson that will lead toward overall session goals.

To prepare the sequence and procedure of each lesson, work backward from the culminating activity of each class.

For example, if the culminating activity is a combination that you have prepared, ask five questions to determine the content and structure of the day's lesson:

- What are the movements that comprise this combination?
- What are the isolations that comprise the movements?
- What are the weight changes or steps in this combination?
- What are the transitions of the combination, such as directional changes or dance positions?
- What are the relevant musical components, such as rhythm, instrumentation or timing, highlighted in the combination?

Teach each of the components of the combination separately in this sequence:
1. **Isolations** - Engage the proper muscles for isolations
2. **Movements** - Combine isolations to create the movements
3. **Steps and Turns** - Add the weight changes, steps and turns
4. **Transitions** - Find and detail the transitions
5. **Music and Aesthetics** - Incorporate the relevant musical elements

Repeat and practice each component several times, then check for understanding by watching students perform the exercise on their own.

Before putting all of the components together for the full combination, check for comprehension by having students perform each component as you watch. Remember the learning objectives of the different levels of students. In the beginner level, you are only checking for comprehension, not for mastery. If you are following this curriculum in the order presented, students will have the opportunity to continually improve their skills in different contexts throughout the year.

When a majority of students appear to understand the concepts, acknowledge the achievement by providing positive feedback. Go forward with putting all the components together for the culminating combination. Be sure to offer honest, helpful and respectful feedback to students throughout the duration of the class.

Throughout the year, use a variety of music to keep students interested and to demonstrate the theme of each session. If your music library is limited, consider adding to it. In addition to the drill routines and choreography songs suggested in each session, I have compiled a list of albums and artists to help expand your music collection for teaching and practice.

The playlists for each lesson are selected from these titles, listed in the Resources section at the end of the book. I have made every effort to include titles that, at the time of the publication of this book, are available on compact disc or digital download from Amazon or iTunes. A Google search of exact song title, and album or artist should point you to a favorable purchase link.

1
Fall Session:
Foundations in Folklore

Pre-requisite for students: none

Learning Goals: Students learn about belly dance movements, music and culture through its folkloric roots.

Technique	Music & Culture	Artistry
• Students will gain or improve body awareness and muscle control through the vocabulary of body isolations • Students will be able to combine body isolations to perform basic belly dance movements and steps	• Students will be able to identify and mark the accented beats of baladi and saidi rhythms with body movements • Students will explore the dance flavors of baladi and saidi styling and cultural context, including maqsoum and fellahi rhythms	• Students will be able to perform a sequence of choreographed drills and combinations in the folkloric styles presented • Students will practice poses and body lines of performance aesthetics to instill confidence

Grading Criteria: Rubrics for Student Evaluation (optional)

Objectives	Needs reinforcement	Solid understanding, benefits from practice	Mastery, enjoys advanced exploration
Improved body awareness and muscle control through the vocabulary of body isolations			
Combine practice of body movements with rhythmic steps			
Identify and mark the accented beats of baladi and saidi rhythms with body movements			
Perform a sequence of choreographed drills and combinations in the folkloric styles presented			
Effort in exploring the dance flavors of baladi and saidi styling and cultural context, including maqsoum and fellahi rhythms			
Confidence in practicing poses and body lines of performance aesthetics to instill confidence.			

Fall Session (Part 1)

Week 1
Isolations | Baladi Rhythm | First, Second & Third Positions

Teaching Objectives:

- Engage students in awareness of weight distribution, foot positions, and function of the joints, such as the knees and elbows

- Introduce and practice body isolations with the concept of muscle engagement

- Prepare students to perform the culminating activity, Isolations Drills sequence to the baladi rhythm

Lower Body Isolations:	**Sample Isolations Drill to Baladi Rhythm**	**Dance Positions:**
- Abdominal contraction - Abdominal release (belly pop) - Hip slide side-to-side - Hip tilt - Glute contraction **Upper Body Isolations:** - Chest lift (upper abs, upper back) - Chest drop - Chest slide (obliques, upper back, upper abs) - Trapezius contraction - Pectoral contraction - Head slides (optional)	**Arabesque pose** (weight on L) 2 cts head slide, pause 2 cts 2 cts R shoulder accent, " 2 cts RL shoulder accent, " 2 cts chest drop, " **Classic belly dance stance** (weight remains on L) 2 cts belly pop on 1AND, pause 3, 4 2 cts R glute contraction/hip tilt 2 cts L glute contraction/hip tilt 2 cts cross R over L (or shift weight L to R) 16cts. Repeat on L (weight on R) **Repeat entire sequence 4x.**	Second position Close the foot to transition First or Third position

Fall Session
Week 1, continued

Procedure | Suggested Playlist

1. Introduction & Warm-up

Fast warm-up	1- "Bahibak Aktar," Amr Diab
Slow warm-up	2- "Hatshepsut reprise," Hatshepsut

Warm-up Isolations:
   Lower abdominal contract/release
   Chest lift, drop
   Ribcage slide, twist
   Shoulder roll
	3- "Sexy Saidi," Drumspyder

Body awareness, alignment, dance positions & muscle engagement	4- "Modern Mystics," Fire Dance

2. Stationary Muscle Engagement & Isolations Exercises

Abdominal contract Abdominal release (belly pop)	5- Maksoum," Arabic Rhythms
Hip slide	6- "Caravan Trek," Sensual Art of Belly Dance: Fast Rhythms
Hip tilt	7- "Bring it Down," The SharQui Workout
Glute contraction	8- "Baladi Seghir," Hatshepsut
Ribcage and shoulder isolations Trapezius and pectoral contraction (neck stretch and head slides, optional)	9- "Saidi," Arabic World Dances
Leg shimmy short drill or prep and/or hip drills, or practice weight shifts	10- "Baladi," Arabic Rhythms

1-2 minute break for water, questions, or comments

3. Movements for New Combination

Practice isolations in the different dance positions	11-"Maqsoum Slow," Tribal Dance Tribal Drums

4. Culminating Activity: Isolations Drill to Masmoudi Saghir, a.k.a. "Baladi" rhythm

Students follow the teacher to perform the Isolations Drill sequence to the baladi rhythm. Repeat 4x or more. **Assessment (optional):** Students perform the culminating activity without the teacher. Teacher may prompt. Advance students may lead.	12- "Balady," The Dancing Drum

5. Final Activity (optional)

Short shimmy or hip drill	13- "Urban Bedu," Repercussion

6. Cool-down & Stretch

Review dance positions and do final stretches	14- "Ocean Depth," Goddess Workout

Fall Session
Week 1, continued

7. Thank and praise your students

Promote a future class, community event, or say something about the topic of the next class. Wish them a wonderful evening, weekend or week, whichever is appropriate.

Reflections:

What went well?

What could have been better?

Did the students' learning behaviors match your expectations?

What would you do differently next time?

Teaching Tip #1

Take a short stretch break after every 2 to 3 songs. Ask how everyone is doing and pay close attention to students with known injuries.

Week 2
Horizontal Movements | Maqsoum Rhythm | Balance & Counter-Balance

Teaching Objectives:

- Guide students in muscle engagement to perform horizontal circular body movements
- Practice the balance and counter-balance of dance positions to help students get into proper body alignment and create beautiful body lines
- Prepare students to perform a 16-count combination

Key Isolations & Movements:	Sample combinations:	Dance Positions:
• Ribcage slide side to side and fwd/back • Horizontal ribcage circle • Hip slide side-to-side and fwd/back • Horizontal Hip Circle	**"Corkscrew" Combo** Ribcage circle, followed by hip circle. **Hip Circle "Spiral" Combo:** 8 cts 1 quarter-time hip circle 4 cts 1 half-time hip circle 4 cts 2 full-time hip circles Repeat other direction. Repeat entire sequence 4x. **For challenge (advanced students):** Ribcage circle and hip circle simultaneously Layer with a lower or upper body shimmy Pivot in place with the combination	First position Start in first position and end in third position.

Fall Session
Week 2, continued

Procedure | Suggested Playlist

1. Introduction & Warm-up

Fast warm-up	1- "Behebak Aktar," Amr Diab
Slow warm-up	2- "Hatshepsut reprise," Hatshepsut

Warm-up Isolations:
    Lower abdominal contract/release
    Chest lift, drop
    Ribcage slide, twist
    Shoulder roll
	3- "Sexy Saidi," Drumspyder

Body awareness, dance positions & muscle engagement	4- "Modern Mystics," Fire Dance

2. Stationary Lower Body & Upper Body Isolations Exercise

Abdominal contract/release	5- "Maksoum," Arabic Rhythms
Hip tilt	6- "Bring it Down," The SharQui Workout
Glute contraction	7- "Baladi Seghir," Hatshepsut
Leg shimmy short drill or prep and/or hip drills, or practice weight shifts	8- "Baladi," Arabic Rhythms
Review Isolations Drill from previous week	9- "Balady," The Dancing Drum

1-2 minute break for water, questions, or comments

3. Movements for New Combination

Horizontal ribcage circle and hip circle	10- "Saidi," Arabic World Dances
Hip slide fwd/back and side to side	11- "Caravan Trek," Sensual Art of Belly Dance: Fast Rhythms

4. Culminating Activity: "Corkscrew" & "Spiral" Combinations

Students follow the teacher to perform the "Corkscrew" and "Spiral" combinations to the maqsoum rhythm **Assessment (optional):** Students perform the combinations without the teacher. Teacher may prompt. Advance students may lead.	12- "Maqsoum Slow," Tribal Dance Tribal Drums

5. Final Activity (optional)

Short shimmy or hip drill	13- "Urban Bedu," Repercussion

6. Cool-down & Stretch

Review dance positions, or other fluid movements, and do final stretches	14- "Ocean Depth," Goddess Workout

Fall Session
Week 2, continued

7. Thank and praise your students

Promote a future class, community event, or say something about the topic of the next class. Wish them a wonderful evening, weekend or week, whichever is appropriate.

Reflections:

What went well?

What could have been better?

Did the students' learning behaviors match your expectations?

What would you do differently next time?

Teaching Tip #2

It is beneficial and enjoyable for students to try many different movements and skills and also to try more advanced concepts. The exception would be if the advanced concept posed the possibility of injury because the students are not properly conditioned. Though much of traditional Middle Eastern dance movements are body-friendly, it is good to note which types of movements may cause or aggravate an injury for some participants.

Movements that require caution include:
- hopping or jumping steps
- level changes or bent knee maneuvers
- repetitive or sharp head movements
- backbends
- pivots and turns

Week 3
Vertical Movements | Maqsoum Rhythm | Weight Shift & Transitions

Teaching Objectives:

- Guide students in muscle engagement, transitions and musical phrasing to perform vertical circular movements, such as hip and ribcage figure eights.

- Prepare students for a sequence of vertical movements in a 16-count combination to the maqsoum rhythm, which will be repeated to complete a 32-count phrase.

Key Isolations & Movements:	Sample Combinations:	Dance Positions:
- Ribcage tilt - Vertical ribcage circle - Hip lift - Hip drop - Vertical Figure 8 **Rock-Step** (Variation of 2-step)	**Figure 8+Hip Drop Combo** 6 cts vertical hip figure 8 (lift to prepare on 7, 8) 8 cts hip drop Repeat other direction. Repeat sequence 4x. **For challenge:** Add tempo variations to the combination, such as quick-quick-slow. **Rock-Step Combination** 2 cts vertical ribcage circle 2 cts horizontal hip circle **For challenge:** Layer ribcage circle with hip circle	Fourth position

Fall Session
Week 3, continued

Procedure | Suggested Playlist

1. Introduction & Warm-up

Fast warm-up	1- "Bahebak Aktar," Amr Diab
Slow warm-up	2- "Hatshepsut reprise," Hatshepsut
Warm-up Isolations: 　Lower abdominal contract/release 　Chest lift, drop 　Ribcage slide, twist 　Shoulder roll	3- "Sexy Saidi," Drumspyder
Body awareness, alignment & muscle engagement	4- "Modern Mystics," Fire Dance

2. Stationary Isolations & Movements

Abdominal contract/release	5- "Maksoum," Arabic Rhythms
Hip tilt/hip lift shifting from first to third positions	6- "Bring it Down," The SharQui Workout
Glute contractions, shifting from first to third positions	7- "Baladi Seghir," Hatshepsut
Leg shimmy short drill or prep and/or hip drills, or practice weight shifts	8- "Baladi," Arabic Rhythms
Review one or more combinations from previous weeks	9- "Caravan Trek," Sensual Art of Belly Dance: Fast Rhythms

1-2 minute break for water, questions, or comments

3. Steps & Movements for New Combination

R Hip drop in third and fourth positions	10- "Maqsoum Baladi," Pulse of the Sphynx
L Hip drop in third and fourth positions	11- "Maqsoum Baladi," Pulse of the Sphynx
Vertical hip figure 8 Rock-step	12- "Saidi," Arabic World Dances

4. Culminating Activity: Vertical movements & Step Combinations

Students follow teacher in performing two combinations:
 	
   Figure 8 + hip drop combination
   Rock-step + ribcage and hip circle combination
 	
"Assessment (optional): Students perform the combinations without the teacher. Teacher may prompt. Advance students may lead.
	13- Maqsoum Slow," Tribal Dance Tribal Drums

5. Final Activity (optional)

Short shimmy or hip drill	14- "Urban Bedu," Repercussion

6. Cool-down & Stretch

Move through dance positions, fluid movements, do final stretches	15- "Ocean Depth," Goddess Workout

Fall Session
Week 3, continued

7. Thank and praise your students

Promote a future class, community event, or say something about the topic of the next class. Wish them a wonderful evening, weekend or week.

Reflections:

What went well?

What could have been better?

Did the students' learning behaviors match your expectations?

What would you do differently next time?

Teaching Tip #3

Don't be in a hurry to jump on new students to correct them. Give them a few weeks to learn their bodies and become acquainted with your personality, teaching style and studio environment. Certainly, if you see someone doing something that you feel is damaging to the body, say something, but try to use positive language without singling anyone out. Remember, people are sensitive and may be working on body and confidence issues, one of the reasons they have joined your class in the first place. You can help them in the process by using nurturing language and encouraging instructions.

Week 4
Saidi Hips & Steps | Saidi Rhythm | Folkloric Essence

Teaching Objectives:

- Impart cultural and geographic knowledge, ie. origin of the saidi rhythm and steps in Upper Egypt. You may mention *tahtib* now or wait until a future lesson.

- Explore the flavors of the steps through upright posture and high arms, along with strong and fluid hip movements.

- Prepare students for a sequence of saidi-style steps in a 16-count combination to the Saidi rhythm, which will appear in a future routine

Key Isolations & Movements:	Sample Saidi Hip Combo 1:	Dance Positions:
• Chest lift, drop and twist	6 cts or 2 measures saidi hip drops (accenting the "doums")	
• Trapezius and pectoral isolation	Step-touch/hip lift on 7, 8. Repeat on other side.	Fourth position
• Shoulder accent down and fwd-back	**Sample Saidi Step Combo 2:**	
• Hip lift and hip drop	8 cts or 4x saidi hop side-to-side (step-touch with knee lift)	
• Knee lift (90 degree angle)	8 cts or 4x saidi hop fwd-back (rock step)	Third position
Steps in Place:	**For challenge:**	
• Step-touch/hip Lift	Add shoulder accents to steps	
• Step-touch/knee lift	Add a pivot to steps (for advanced students)	
• Rock-step Fwd-Back		

Fall Session
Week 4, continued

Procedure | Suggested Playlist

1. Introduction & Warm-up

Fast warm-up	1- "Behebak Aktar," Amr Diab
Slow warm-up	2- "Hatshepsut reprise," Hatshepsut
Warm-up isolations, marking the saidi rhythm: chest drop, shoulder drop accents down	3- "Sexy Saidi," Drumspyder
Body awareness, dance positions & muscle engagement	4- "Modern Mystics," Fire Dance

2. Stationary Isolations Exercises & Movements

Abdominal contract/release	5- "Maksoum," Arabic Rhythms
Hip tilt/hip lift, shifting from first to third positions	6- "Bring it Down," The SharQui Workout
Glute contractions, shifting from first to third positions	7- "Baladi Seghir," Hatshepsut
Leg shimmy short drill or prep and/or hip drills, or practice weight shifts	8- "Baladi," Arabic Rhythms

1-2 minute break for water, questions, or comments

3. Steps & Movements for New Combination

R saidi hip drop in third and fourth positions	9- "Saidi Slow," Pulse of the Sphynx
L saidi hip drop in third and fourth positions	10- "Saidi Slow," Pulse of the Sphynx
Alternating saidi hip drops R to L, step-touch to change sides on count 3 of fourth measure (optional)	11. "Saidi Slow," Pulse of the Sphynx
Review hip figure 8 combo from previous week with saidi hip drops	12- "Saidi," Arabic World Dances
Review rock-step combo from previous week. Introduce step-touch with knee lift (hop)	13- Saidi Lento" Todos Los Ritmos Arabes

4. Culminating Activity: Saidi Combinations

Saidi hip and step combinations **Assessment (optional):** Students perform the combinations without the teacher. Teacher may prompt. Advance students may lead.	14- "Saidi Lento," Todos Los Ritmos Arabes
	15- "Saidi Rapido," Todos Los Ritmos Arabes

5. Final Activity (optional)

Short shimmy or hip drill	16- "Urban Bedu," Repercussion

6. Cool-down & Stretch

Review dance positions and fluid movements, and do final stretches	17- "Ocean Depth," Goddess Workout

Fall Session
Week 4, continued

7. Thank and praise your students

Promote a future class, community event, or say something about the topic of the next class. Wish them a wonderful evening, weekend or week.

Reflections:

What went well?

What could have been better?

Did the students' learning behaviors match your expectations?

What would you do differently next time?

 Teaching Tip #4

Before introducing movements for a specific rhythm, introduce the rhythm first and have students clap the accented beats or "Doums." Then introduce the corresponding movements.

Week 5
Saidi Step Combinations | Saidi Rhythm | Folkloric Essence

Teaching Objectives

- Share additional cultural and geographic knowledge about saidi dance and music, or folkloric dance in general. Key points to mention may include costuming and props such as tahtib/assaya, baladi dresses
- Expose students to the flavor of saidi dance and music through saidi-style combinations
- Prepare student to perform steps and combinations that will appear in a future choreography

Key Isolations & Movements:	Sample Saidi Combination:	Dance Positions:
• Chest lift, drop and twist • Trapezius and pectoral isolation • Shoulder accent down and fwd-back • Shoulder shimmy • Hip tilt, slide • Hip lift and hip drop • Knee lift (90 degree angle) **Steps in Place:** • Step-touch and step-lift (knee) • Rock-step fwd-back	8 cts or 4x saidi hop side-to-side (step-touch with knee lift) with shoulder drop accents 8 cts or 4x saidi hop fwd-back (rock step) with shoulder fwd-back accents or shimmy 8 cts or 4 vertical figure 8 8 cts or 2 measures saidi hip drops (or 8 steady hip drops for easier version) Repeat 2x. **Alternate version (more challenging):** 4cts of each step. Repeat 4x.	Fourth position Third position

Fall Session
Week 5, continued

Procedure | Suggested Playlist

1. Introduction & Warm-up

Fast warm-up	1- "Behebak Aktar," Amr Diab
Slow warm-up	2- "Hatshepsut reprise," Hatshepsut

Warm-up isolations, marking the saidi rhythm:
    Chest drop
    Shoulder drop accent down
	3- "Sexy Saidi," Drumspyder

Body Awareness, Dance Positions & Muscle Engagement	4- "Modern Mystics," Fire Dance

2. Stationary Isolation Exercises & Movements

Upper body isolations	5- "Maksoum," Arabic Rhythms
Hip tilt/lift/drop shifting from first to third positions	6- "Bring it Down," The SharQui Workout
Glute contractions, shifting from first to third positions	7- "Baladi Seghir," Hatshepsut
Leg shimmy short drill or prep and/or hip drills, or practice weight shifts	8- Baladi," Arabic Rhythms

1-2 minute break for water, questions, or comments

3. Steps & Movements for New Combination

Review saidi hip drop combos	9- "Saidi Slow," Pulse of the Sphynx
	10 - "Saidi Slow," Pulse of the Sphynx
Review hip figure 8 combo with saidi hip drops	11- "Saidi," Arabic World Dances
Review rock-step combo from week 3 Introduce step-touch with knee lift (hop)	12- "Saidi Lento" Todos Los Ritmos Arabes

4. Culminating Activity: More Saidi Combinations

Students follow the teacher in performing the saidi hip and step combinations **"Assessment (optional):** Students perform the combinations without the teacher. Teacher may prompt. Advance students may lead.	13- "Saidi Lento"
	14- Saidi Rapido," Todos Los Ritmos Arabes

5. Final Activity (optional)

Short shimmy or hip drill	15- "Urban Bedu," Repercussion

Fall Session
Week 5, continued

6. Cool-down & Stretch

Review dance position or other fluid movements, and do final stretches	16- "Ocean Depth," Goddess Workout

7. Thank and praise your students

Promote a future class, community event, or say something about the topic of the next class. Wish them a wonderful evening, weekend or week.

Reflections:

What went well?

What could have been better?

Did the students' learning behaviors match your expectations?

What would you do differently next time?

Teaching Tip #5

As you follow the curriculum and session plans, it is important to always begin with the most basic form of the lesson's concepts before moving onward to the lesson objectives. Do not skip any foundational material. New and returning dancers require the same strong foundation in order to advance their skills and have a safe and enjoyable dance experience.

Week 6
Saidi Drill Choreography, "Ala Nar"

Teaching Objectives:

- Incorporate key movements and steps from the previous lesson into a drill choreography
- Combine the characteristic saidi steps in a simple and easy to follow sequence to a well-known traditional saidi song, **Ala Nar**, which translates to "on fire."

Suggested Steps	Music Breakdown	Drill Routine to "Ala Nar"
• Step-Touch/hip lift	**Intro**	Create a simple and easy to follow drills-based choreography.
• Step-Touch/knee lift	**(1)** :10, 8cts x 4	
• Pulsing-hip slide, pulsing hip circle	**(2)** :27, 8cts x 4	
	(3) :43, 8cts x 3, Repeat	
• Vertical hip figure 8	1:09, Same as **(1)**	
• Hip drop (basic or with saidi accent)	1:25, Same as **(2)**	
	1:42, Same as **(3)**	
• Said hop side to side with shoulder accents	2:05 8cts x 3	
• Rock step fwd-back with shoulder shimmy	2:19, Same as **(1)**	
	2:35, Same as **(2)**	
	2:51 Same as **(3)**	
	Fade out	

Fall Session
Week 6, continued

Procedure | Suggested Playlist

1. Introduction & Warm-up

Fast warm-up	1- "Behebak Aktar," Amr Diab
Slow warm-up	2- "Hatshepsut reprise," Hatshepsut

Warm-up isolations marking the saidi rhythm:
    Chest drop
    Shoulder drop accent down
	3- "Sexy Saidi," Drumspyder

Body awareness, dance positions & muscle engagement	4- "Modern Mystics," Fire Dance

2. Stationary Isolation Exercises & Movements

Abdominal contraction Hip slide	5- "Maksoum," Arabic Rhythms
Hip tilt/lift/drop shifting from first to third positions	6- "Bring it Down," The SharQui Workout
Glute contractions, shifting from first to third positions	7- "Baladi Seghir," Hatshepsut

1-2 minute break for water, questions, or comments

3. Review & Build-up of Combinations for Drill Choreography

Heel pulse Rock-step fwd/back, side to side	8-"Saidi Slow," Pulse of the Sphynx
Saidi hip drops	9- "Saidi Slow," Pulse of the Sphynx
Hip circle Pulsing hip circle Vertical hip figure 8	10- "Saidi," Arabic World Dances
Practice individual steps at this faster tempo	11- "Saidi Rapido" Todos Los Ritmos Arabes
Introduce and practice combinations for "Ala Nar" drill choreography	12- "Bent elAosool," Oriental Belly Dance Vol. 2: Darbouka and Tabla

4. Culminating Activity: "Ala Nar" Drill Choreography

Students follow the teacher to perform the drill choreography	13- "Ala Nar," Beyond the Desert: Classical Egyptian Belly Dance
Assessment (optional): Students perform the choreography without the teacher. Teacher may prompt. Advance students may lead.	Repeat as time allows

5. Cool-down & Stretch

Perform fluid movements and do final stretches	14- "Ocean Depth," Goddess Workout

**Fall Session
Week 6, continued**

6. *Thank and praise your students.*

Promote a future class, community event, or say something about the topic of the next class. Wish them a wonderful evening, weekend or week.

Reflections:

What went well?

What could have been better?

Did the students' learning behaviors match your expectations?

What would you do differently next time?

Teaching Tip #6

Use simple choreography as a tool to build dynamic drills to reinforce movements or demonstrate other concepts. It is not necessary for students to memorize the drill choreography or master the concepts, though some may. Design it to be easy to follow and to provide practice. Keep it simple and have fun!

Fall Session (Part 2)

Week 1 or 7
Isolations & Movements Drill Routine, "The Arabic Party"

Teaching Objective:

- Guide students in performing isolations in different dance positions with proper alignment and muscle engagement
- Teach a dynamic drills-based choreography incorporating isolations, musical timing, phrasing, weight changes and dance positions ("The Arabic Party," Oriental Belly Dance Vol. 2: Darbouka and Tabla)
- Prepare students to perform the combinations of the drill routine with an emphasis on muscle engagement, transitions and weight changes

Isolations:	Suggested Music: "The Arabic Party"	Poses and stance

• Hip Slide
• Glute contractions
• Trapezius and pectoral contractions
• Ribcage lift and twist
 	
Movements & Articulations:
• Hip sway
• Hip lift
• Hip drop
• Shoulder shimmy (optional)
 	
Suggested Steps:
• Step-touch
• Step-touch/hip lift
• Step-touch/knee lift
	Intro
	(1) :24 8cts x 4 + 8cts x 4
	(2) 1:02 4cts x 4
	(3) 1:11 8cts x 4
	(4) 1:27 8cts + 8cts x 4
	1:48 Repeat **(2)**
	1:57 Repeat **(3)**
	2:13 Repeat **(4)**
	2:34 Repeat **(2)**
	(5) 2:42 8ct x 2
	      8cts x 4
	      8cts x 4
	      8cts x 4
	3:32 Repeat **(3)**
	3:49 Repeat **(4)**
	4:10 Repeat **(2)**
	4:18 Repeat **(3)**
	4:35 Repeat **(4)**
	5:04 Similar to **(5)**
	      8ct x 2
	      8cts x 4
	      8cts x 4
	      8cts x 2 End
		Weight shifted movements
		
		Second and third positions

Fall Session (Part 2)
Week 1 or 7, continued

Procedure | Suggested Playlist

1. Introduction & Warm-up

Fast warm-up	1- "Bellydance," Bellydance Superstars, Vol 5
Slow warm-up	2- "Hatshepsut reprise," Hatshepsut

Warm-up Isolations:
    Abdominal contract and release
    Chest lift
    Trapezius and pectoral contraction
    Ribcage twist
	3- "Sexy Saidi," The Nekyia Vol. 1

Body awareness, dance positions & muscle engagement	4- "Modern Mystics," Fire Dance

2. Stationary Weight-Shifted Isolations & Movements

Isolations in first position: hip slide, hip tilt	5- "Caravan Trek," Sensual Art of Belly Dance: Fast Rhythms
Isolations in second position: glute contraction, hip lift	6- "Shimmy," Belly Dance Music
Isolations in third position: glute contraction, hip twist	7- "Saidi III," Arabic Rhythms
Shimmy practice (short)	8- "Moon Dance," Sensual Art of Belly Dance: Fast Rhythms

1-2 minute break for water, questions, or comments

3. Review & Practice of Key Movements

R Hip lift with glute contraction right on the downbeat: half-time, full time, double time	9- "Ayoub Simple," Pulse of the Sphynx
R Hip drop with glute contraction left on the downbeat: half-time, full time, double time	10- "Ayoub Simple," Pulse of the Sphynx
L Hip lift with glute contraction right on the downbeat: half-time, full time, double time	11- "Maqsoum baladi," Pulse of the Sphynx
L Hip drop with glute contraction left on the downbeat: half-time, full time, double time	12- "Maqsoum baladi," Pulse of the Sphynx
Review "Ala Nar" drill choreography from previous week (optional)	13- "Ala Nar," Beyond the Desert: Classical Egyptian Belly Dance Music

4. Culminating Activity: Drill Choreography, "The Arabic Party," Build-Up of Combinations & Transitions

Review and practice combinations of the drill routine with emphasis on transitions and weight changes	14- "Bent ElAosool," Oriental Belly Dance Vol. 2: Darbouka and Tabla
Students follow the teacher to perform drill sequence of isolations and basic movements. **Assessment (optional):** Students perform key parts of the drill choreography without the teacher. Teacher may prompt. Advance students may lead.	15- "The Arabic Party," Oriental Belly Dance Vol. 2: Darbouka and Tabla

Fall Session (Part 2)
Week 1 or 7, continued

5. Cool-down & Stretch

Perform fluid movements and do final stretches	16- "Ocean Depth," Goddess Workout

6. Thank and praise your students.

Promote a future class, community event, or say something about the topic of the next class. Wish them a wonderful evening, weekend or week.

Reflections:

What went well?

What could have been better?

Did the students' learning behaviors match your expectations?

What would you do differently next time?

Teaching Tip #7

Students need and want you to be confident and in charge. This makes their class experience safe and fun. Ask for feedback from students and consider their comments and suggestions. But not everyone's suggestion needs to be implemented or taken personally. Remember, you are in charge of creating an environment that benefits everyone, not just one or two.

Week 2 or 8
Shimmies | Tempos & Timing | Maqsoum (fast tempo) & Fellahi Rhythms

Teaching Objectives:

- Introduce 2 to 4 shimmies or variations and coordinating musical flavors
- Emphasize the freedom and liberation of shimmies while guiding students to stay in proper alignment
- Explore the tempos of the individual movements of shimmies in half time, full time and double-time
- Distinguish between hip and leg shimmy, shoulder and chest shimmy

Key Isolations & Movements	Suggested Drill Sequence:	Dance Positions:
• Hip tilt	8cts shoulder shimmy	First position
• Ribcage twist	8cts leg shimmy	
• Trapezius contraction	8cts hip shimmy	
• Pectoral contraction	8ct weight-shifted leg shimmy	Second or third position
• Shoulder accent		
Shimmies:	Reverse order and repeat.	
• Shoulder shimmy	Repeat 4cts each	
• 4/4 Hip shimmy (oblique-driven)	**3/4 Shimmy drill:**	
• 4/4 Leg shimmy (quad-driven)	Begin with quarter time and half time	
• 3/4 shimmy down or up	**For challenge:**	
	Progress to full time and double time	
	Add small traveling steps and patterns	

Fall Session (Part 2)
Week 2 or 8, continued

Procedure | Suggested Playlist

1. Introduction & Warm-up

Procedure	Suggested Playlist
Fast warm-up	1- "Bellydance," Bellydance Superstars, Vol 5
Slow warm-up	2- "Hatshepsut reprise," Hatshepsut

Warm-up Isolations:
    Abdominal contract and release
    Chest lift
    Trapezius and pectoral contraction
    Ribcage twist
	3- "Sexy Saidi," The Nekyia Vol. 1

Body awareness, alignment & muscle engagement with focus on knees and pelvis	4- "Caravan Trek," Sensual Art of Belly Dance

2. Stationary Isolation Exercises for Shimmies

Procedure	Suggested Playlist

Slow tempo:
    Hip slide
    Hip tilt (weight-centered)
	5- "Caravan Trek," Sensual Art of Belly Dance

Faster tempo:
    Hip slide
    Hip tilt
	6- "Maqsoum," Pulse of the Sphynx

Leg shimmy practice: Emphasize the gentle knee motion, and relaxing the legs and buttocks.	7- "Baladi," Arabic Rhythms
Shoulder shimmy	8- "Full Moon Ritual," Goddess Workout

1-2 minute break for water, questions, or comments

3. Culminating Activity: Shimmy Drills

Basic 4/4 hip shimmy: 　　Half time 　　Full time 　　Double time	9- "Stamina," Fate
Shoulder shimmy, chest shimmy	
Leg/knee shimmy	
Combo drill with hip, shoulder and leg/knee shimmy	
3/4 shimmy: 　　Half time 　　Full time 　　Double time 　　Add traveling for challenge	
As time allows: 　　Alternate drills and shimmies 　　Practice layering lower body shimmies with hip slides, snake arms, and ribcage circles 　　Practice layering upper body shimmies with chest lifts, step-touch, and ribcage circles	

5. Cool-down & Stretch

Review dance positions, perform fluid movements, and do final stretches	10- "Modern Mystics," Fire Dance
	11- "Ocean Depth," Goddess Workout

6. Thank and praise your students.

Promote a future class, community event, or say something about the topic of the next class. Wish them a wonderful evening, weekend or week.

Reflections:

What went well?

What could have been better?

Did the students' learning behaviors match your expectations?

What would you do differently next time?

Teaching Tip #8

Create a custom play list of appropriate music to follow the format of your class exactly. If, during the lesson, you need to pause and explain something in advance, add a 1 to 2 minute track that is slow and soft to give you time to talk. When the track ends, move on to the activity.

Week 3 or 9
Upper Body, Arms, Pivots | Saidi, Maqsoum and/or Baladi Rhythms

Teaching Objectives:

- Practice basic movements and previous steps (if appropriate) with a focus on upper body carriage, arm frames and transitions
- Introduce and practice snake arm movement leading with ribcage articulation
- Introduce the concept of direction changes with 1/8 and 1/4 pivot turns

Key Isolations & Movements	Arm Frames and Transitions:	Dance positions:
• Ribcage slide, twist and tilt • Hip lift and drop • Horizontal and vertical ribcage figure 8 • Arm frames, positions and transitions with foot positions **Pivots:** • 1/8 pivot turn • 1/4 pivot turn	Hip drops w/diagonal arms Shoulder accents and shimmies Snake arms with shimmy layer (shimmy optional, add as a challenge) Transitions and direction changes with horizontal and vertical ribcage figure 8 Explore arm paths. Layer shimmy with arm movements for challenge.	Third position First position Second position (Arabesque)

Fall Session (Part 2)
Week 3 or 9, continued

Procedure | Suggested Playlist

1. Introduction & Warm-up

Fast warm-up	1- "Bellydance," Bellydance Superstars Vol. 5
Slow warm-up	2- "Hatshepsut," Hapshepsut

Warm-up Isolations
    Abdominal contractions
    Ribcage lift and slide
    Trapezius and pectoral contraction
	3- "Sexy Saidi," The Nekyia Vol. 1

Body awareness, alignment & muscle engagement	4- "Modern Mystics," Fire Dance

2. Stationary Isolation Exercises & Articulations

Isolations and movements in different dance positions:
    Glute contraction
    Hip slide
    Hip sway
    Hip lift, drop
	5- "Caravan Trek," Sensual Art of Belly Dance: Fast Rhythms

Ribcage lift, drop slide and twist Trapezius and pectoral contraction	6- "Maqsoum slow," Tribal Dance Tribal Drums
Arm paths, transitions in the dance positions with different movements	7- "Source of Nectar," Goddess Workout

1-2 minute break for water, questions, or comments

3. New Combinations & Steps

Horizontal ribcage figure 8 Vertical ribcage figure 8	8- "Dance Dolphin Dance," Goddess Workout
Snake arms	9- "Saidi," Arabic World Dances

Practice simple steps and pivots incorporating arm paths and transitions in the dance positions with different movements
    1/8 pivot step
    1/4 pivot step
	10- "El Hombre el Saidi," Flamenco Arabe 2

4. Culminating Activity: Combinations or Drills for Elegant Arms & Body Carriage

Students follow the teacher to perform drills or combinations incorporating arm movements and body carriage with direction changes. **Assessment (optional):** Students perform the culminating activity without the teacher. Advanced students may lead.	11- "Ala Nar" Beyond the Desert: Classical Egyptian Belly Dance Music
	12- "The Arabic Party," Oriental Belly Dance Vol. 2: Darbouka and Tabla

6. Cool-down & Stretch

Perform fluid movements and do final stretches	13- "Ocean Depth," Goddess Workout

Fall Session (Part 2)
Week 3 or 9, continued

7. Thank and praise your students.

Promote a future class, community event, or say something about the topic of the next class. Wish them a wonderful evening, weekend or week.

Reflections:

What went well?

What could have been better?

Did the students' learning behaviors match your expectations?

What would you do differently next time?

Teaching Tip #9

You may be tempted to use a hands-on approach to correct some students. Always ask permission before you touch a student. But keep in mind that some students may give consent for fear of being impolite, or feel intimidated, when in reality they do not actually like to be touched. It is better to get to know students first before attempting to use hands-on approach of correction. You never know what will trigger the fight or flight response, especially in students who have experienced trauma or abuse.

Week 4 or 10
Folkloric-Style Combinations | Saidi & Maqsoum Rhythms

Teaching Objectives:

- Introduce the half time walk as the basis for many folkloric style steps, and the folkloric four-step with variations and transitions
- Practice drills that incorporate movements, pivots and traveling steps that will appear in a saidi-style choreography
- Emphasize the diversity of belly dance movements derived from folkloric roots

Key Isolations & Movements:	Suggested Practice Drills	Dance Positions:
- Hip tilt - Hip sway - Shoulder shimmy **Steps:** - Heel pulse - Four-step - Traveling hip sway - 1/8 and 1/4 pivot turn	**Combination 1:** 8 cts (4x) four-step with shoulder shimmy, transition to other side on 7, 8 Repeat to other side **Combination 2:** 8 cts (4 steps) half time hip sway traveling forward Repeat traveling back pulsing shoulders down and extending the leg (no hip) **For challenge:** Add a 3/4 hip shimmy (half time) to each forward step Add 1/8 or 1/4 pivot to each backward step	Fourth position Third position

Fall Session (Part 2)
Week 4 or 10, continued

Procedure | Suggested Playlist

1. Introduction & Warm-up

Fast warm-up	1- "Bellydance," Bellydance Superstars, Vol. 5
Slow warm-up	2- "Hatshepsut reprise," Hatshepsut

Warm-up Isolations:
    Abdominal contraction
    Hip slide
    Ribcage lift, slide, twist
    Shoulder drop accent
    Shoulder roll
	3- "Sexy Saidi," The Nekyia, Vol. 1

Dance positions for folkloric dance:
    Heel pulse (calf raises)
    Leg extension
    Ball-to-heel stepping technique
	4- "Modern Mystics," Fire Dance

2. Stationary Isolation Exercises & Articulations

Hip tilt Glute contraction	5- "Bring it Down," The SharQui Workout
Hip sway	6- "Baladi seghir," Hatshepsut
Review Isolations Drill	7- "The Arabic Party," Oriental Belly Dance, Vol. 2: Darabouka and Tabla

1-2 minute break for water, questions, or comments

3. Movements for New Saidi Combinations

From suggested combination:
    Half time traveling hip sway forward
    Half time traveling step heel pulse backward
    Add 1/8 and 1/4 pivot turn to each step
Slow and fast tempos
	8- "Maqsoum slow," Tribal Dance Tribal Drums

	9- "Maksoum," The Dancing Drum

4-step with: (Lead R foot then L)
    Shoulder shimmy
    Ribcage lift
 	
Additional combination (optional):
    4 cts Rock-step with shoulder or chest shimmy
    4 cts Step-lift knee with shoulder drop accents
	10- "El Hombre el Saidi," Flamenco Arabe 2

4. Culminating Activity: New Saidi Combinations

Students follow the teacher to perform the new saidi-style step combinations in a sequence.	11- "Saidi lento," Todos los Ritmos Arabes
Assessment (optional): Students perform the culminating activity without the teacher. Advanced students may lead.	12- "Saidi rapido," Todos los Ritmos Arabes

5. Final Activity

Short shimmy practice drill	13- "Marhaba," Rough Guide to Belly Dance (First Edition)

Fall Session (Part 2)
Week 4 or 10, continued

6. Cool-down & Stretch

Perform fluid movements and do final stretches	14- "Ocean Depth," Goddess Workout

7. Thank and praise your students.

Promote a future class, community event, or say something about the topic of the next class. Wish them a wonderful evening, weekend or week.

Reflections:

    What went well?

    What could have been better?

    Did the students' learning behaviors match your expectations?

    What would you do differently next time?

Teaching Tip #10

Remember, modern belly dance is derived from social and folk dances that are performed by everyone, including men, women and children. Emphasize this aspect of community and celebration, especially when working with folkloric topics or group choreography.

Week 5 or 11
Saidi Hip Combinations | Saidi Rhythm | Melodic Interpretation

Teaching Objectives:

- Introduce students to a new step combination from the choreography
- Guide students in practice of the combinations with emphasis on transitions and timing
- Draw attention to the melodic instruments in saidi music to inspire fluid, controlled and relaxed movements of the hips and shoulders

Key Isolations & Movements	Suggested Combination:	Dance Positions:
• Hip slide side to side, fwd and back • Hip twist • Glute contraction • Saidi hip drop • Shoulder or chest shimmy **Steps:** • Step-touch • Step-pivot 1/8 • Step-close-step	4 cts step-close-step lateral travel R with horizontal hip circle. Repeat 4x 2 measures saidi hip drops, step-hip pivot 1/8 to transition 2 measure saidi hip drops on other side Shimmy 4 to 8cts Repeat on other side Practice slow and fast tempo	Second, Third and fourth positions Elegant lifted arms and transitions

Fall Session (Part 2)
Week 5 or 11, continued

Procedure | Suggested Playlist

1. Introduction & Warm-up

Fast warm-up	1- "Bellydance, Bellydance Superstars, Vol. 5
Slow warm-up	2- "Hatshepsut," Hatshepsut

Warm-up Isolations
    Abdominal contraction
    Ribcage lift, twist
    Trapezius and pectoral contraction
	3- "Sexy Saidi," The Nekyia Vol. 1

Dance positions for folkloric dance:
    Heel pulse (calf raises)
    Leg extension and knee lift
    Ball-to-heel stepping technique
	4- "Modern Mystics," Fire Dance

2. Stationary Isolation Exercises & Articulations

Hip tilt Glute contraction Hip sway	5- "Baladi seghir," Hatshepsut
Hip slide side to side, fwd and back Shoulder drop accent Shoulder shimmy	6- "Maqsoum slow," Tribal Dance Tribal Drums
Review "Ala Nar" drill choreography	7- "Ala Nar," Beyond the Desert: Classical Egyptian Dance Music

1-2 minute break for water, questions, or comments

3. Movements for New Combinations & Steps

Horizontal hip circle with weight shift
    "   Pivot 360° in 16 cts
    "   Step-close-step
	8- "Saidi," Arabic World Dances

Saidi hip drop, step-pivot transition	9- "Saidi lento," Todos los Ritmos Arabes
Faster tempo	10- Saidi rapido," Todos los Ritmos Arabes

4. Culminating Activity: Drills & Combinations

Students follow the teacher to perform the saidi combination with hip circle and pivots. Review previous week's saidi combination if appropriate. **Assessment (optional):** Students perform the culminating activity without the teacher. Advanced students may lead.	11- "El Hombre el Saidi," Flamenco Arabe
	12- "Nourhan's Baladi," Nourhan's Raqs Sharqi Vol. 1

5. Final Activity

Short shimmy practice drill	13 – "Marhaba," Rough Guide to Belly Dance (First Edition)

6. Cool-down & Stretch

Perform fluid movements and do final stretches	14 – "Ocean Depth," Goddess Workout

Fall Session (Part 2)
Week 5 or 11, continued

7. Thank and praise your students.

Promote a future class, community event, or say something about the topic of the next class. Wish them a wonderful evening, weekend or week.

Reflections:

What went well?

What could have been better?

Did the students' learning behaviors match your expectations?

What would you do differently next time?

Teaching Tip #11

To help students become acquainted with the instruments of Arabic music, look for pictures online and print them out to show and tell in class. You may consider compiling the pictures in a 3-ring binder for easy storage and display.

Week 6 or 12
Saidi Choreography "Saidi Ya Wad"

Teaching Objectives:

- Prepare students for a simple yet fast tempo saidi-style choreography incorporating the movements introduced throughout the session

Suggested Steps:	Music Breakdown:	*Choreography to "Saidi Ya Wad"
- Half time hip sway-pivot forward 4x - Step-touch walk back 4x (For challenge: Step-pulse-kick –pivot with shoulder drop accent) - Four-step on the diagonal (For challenge: Add shoulder shimmies) - Step-close-step with hip circle - Saidi hip drops, step-pivot transition - 4/4 Shimmy - Repeat from the beginning starting on other side - Shimmy to end	**Intro** (1) :08, 8 ct x 4 (2) :25, 8 ct x 4 :41, 8 cts x 4 Repeat (1) (3) :58, 4 ct x 3 (4) 1:05, 4 cts x 4 1:13, 8 cts x 4 Repeat (1) 1:35, 8cts x 4 Repeat (2) 1:48, 8cts x 4 Repeat (1) 4 cts x 4 **End**	Create a simple and easy to follow choreography using the movements and combinations covered in the session.

Fall Session (Part 2)
Week 6 or 12, continued

Procedure | Suggested Playlist

1. Introduction & Warm-up

Fast warm-up	1- "Bellydance," Bellydance Superstars Vol. 5
Slow warm-up	2- "Hatshepsut reprise," Hatshepsut

Warm-up Isolations
    Abdominal contraction
    Ribcage lift, twist
    Trapezius and pectoral contraction
	3- "Sexy Saidi," The Nekyia Vol. 1

Body awareness, alignment & muscle engagement	4- "Modern Mystics," Fire Dance

2. Review and Practice of Key Movements and Combinations

Hip tilt Glute contraction	5- "Baladi seghir," Hatshepsut
Hip sway travel + pivot Four-step + shoulder shimmy Side-step + hip circle Saidi drops	6- "Maqsoum slow," Tribal Dance Tribal Drums
Shimmy Review combinations	7- "Bent ElAosool," Oriental Belly Dance Vol. 2: Darbouka and Tabla
Review Isolations Drill from week 1	8- "Arabic Party," Oriental Belly Dance Vol. 2: Darbouka and Tabla
Review Saidi-style drill choreography	9- "Ala Nar

1-2 minute break for water, questions, or comments

3. Build-up of Combinations & Steps for Choreography

4x half time hip sway forward 4x half time step-touch or kick/pivot with shoulder drop accent backward	10- "Saidi lento," Todos los Ritmos Arabes
8cts four-step with shoulder shimmy on the diagonal, transition on 7, 8 to other side. Side step (step-close-step) hip circle + saidi hip drop combination	11- "Saidi rapido," Todos los Ritmos Arabes

4. Culminating Activity: "Saidi Ya Wad" Choreography

Students follow the teacher to perform the saidi choreography incorporating folkloric style steps and movements. **Assessment (optional):** Students perform the culminating activity without the teacher. Advanced students may lead.	12 – "Saidi Ya Wad," Cairo Plus
	Repeat as time allows

5. Final Activity

Short shimmy practice drill	13- "Marhaba," Rough Guide to Belly Dance (First Edition)

6. Cool-down & Stretch

Perform fluid movements and do final stretches	14 – "Ocean Depth," Goddess Workout

7. Thank and praise your students.

Remind students to sign up for the next session. Tell them a little about what you have planned. Wish them a wonderful evening, weekend or week.

Reflections:

How did the session go for you?

What did you learn about your students?

What would you do differently next time?

Teaching Tip #12

This would be a good time to get formal feedback from your students. A short questionnaire is a great way to collect honest and useful feedback. Keep it simple by using check boxes to rate their experience in your class. You can also include a few short answer questions.

Questions can include:

    Did the class meet your needs and interests?

    Was the instructor knowledgeable about the subject matter?

    Was the instructor prepared for class?

    What did you enjoy most?

    What did you enjoy less?

Regardless of the answers, remember, they are expressing their opinion from their own experience. One student's negative answer may not mean much overall, but you never know when it offers insight and an opportunity to learn. Pay attention to every answer. It does not mean you should try to please everyone. When a student gives you a negative yet valid and honest review, think of it as a gift. If you always did everything right, you would never learn and grow. Focus on your strengths. Learn from your mistakes.

2

Winter Session:
Music & Choreography

Pre-requisite for students: none

Learning Goals: Students learn about Egyptian rhythms, instruments, and choreographic concepts through a classic belly dance choreography: **"Zeina,"** from Bellydance Superstars, Volume 1 (many other versions are widely available). In addition students will be exposed to a variety of music.

A wide range of abilities is to be expected when working with performance-style choreography. Some students may struggle more than others. It is important to emphasize that choreography, in the context of this unit, is a tool for learning about musicality, transitions and artistry, not to require mastery or memorization.

If the choreography is to be performed for an audience, separate rehearsals should be held and mandatory for performing students. Rehearsal time, not class time, should be used to polish a dance for performance.

Winter Session (Part 1)

Technique	Music & Culture	Artistry
• Students will gain or improve body awareness and muscle control through the vocabulary of body isolations. • Students will be able to combine basic movements and steps in a fluid sequence • Students will explore a variety of percussive and fluid movements	• Students will explore a variety of music and rhythms and coordinating movements • Students will be able to identify and mark the accented beats of baladi and ayoub rhythms with body movements and traveling steps • Students will explore the flavor of classic belly dance music and begin to recognize popular songs • Student will be able to recognize instrumental and rhythmic changes in Arabic music	• Students gain confidence by learning a choreography in the classical song presented • Students will gain an understanding of transitions in choreography • Students will gain a basic understanding of musicality in Oriental dance

Grading Criteria: Rubrics for Student Evaluation (optional)

Objectives	Needs reinforcement	Solid understanding, benefits from practice	Mastery, enjoys advanced exploration
Improved body awareness and muscle control through the vocabulary of body isolations			
Effort in exploring a variety of percussive and fluid movements			
Effort in exploring a variety of music and rhythms and coordinating movements			
Identify and mark the accented beats of baladi and ayoub rhythms with body movements and traveling steps			
Recognize instrumental and rhythmic changes in Arabic music			
Recognize instrumental and rhythmic changes in Arabic music			
Confidence in performing choreography in the classical song presented			
Effort in exploring a variety of percussive and fluid movements			
Understanding of transitions in choreography			
Understanding of musicality in Oriental dance			

Winter Session

Week 1
Muscle Engagement & Body Isolations | Baladi or Maqsoum Rhythm | Music Variety

Teaching Objective:

- Engage students in kinesthetic awareness and muscle control through core isolation exercises
- Introduce students to the concept of coordinated sequential body movement and prepare them to perform undulations by conditioning the proper muscle groups
- Create a drill sequence incorporating key movements and isolations: hip sway, hip lift, abdominal, chest and shoulder isolations

*Contract and Release Floor Exercises (Repeat every class for 4-6 weeks)
   Lower Abs/lower back (pelvic floor)
   Mid-Abs/mid-back
   Upper Abs/upper back
   Glute contraction
   Trapezius contraction
   Pectoral contraction
   Should accent/shimmy
   Chest lift
 	
Standing Isolations & Movements
   Hip tilt, hip lift
   Hip slide
   Hip sway
 	
Weight Shift
Transition smoothly from R to L, L to R
	Isolations Drill:
	
	Hip sway
	
	Hip lift
	
	Lower abdominal accent out, aka belly pop
	
	Chest lifts
	
	Chest drops
	
	Shoulder roll into shoulder shimmy
		Dance positions:
		
		First position
		
		Second position
		
		Third position

*These exercises are to be performed sitting on the floor with legs extended and relaxed to help students better identify and condition the core muscles. Be aware that some students may not be comfortable sitting on the floor, or may have difficulty getting back up. Use your best judgment whether to do the exercise sitting or standing. If you choose to do the exercise on the floor, recommend that students bring a yoga mat or towel.

Procedure | Suggested Playlist

1. Introduction & Warm-up

Fast warm-up	1- "Sultana el Houb," Middle Eastern Dance: 30 Hits of Belly Dance
Slow warm-up	2- "Hatshepsut," Hatshepsut

Muscle Engagement Floor Exercises:
    Lower Abs/lower back
    Mid-Abs/mid-back
    Upper Abs/upper back (chest lift)
    Reverse order of contractions
	3- "Whisper," Amir Sofi: Amir

Ribcage twist Trapezius contraction Pectoral contraction Shoulder accents, roll and shimmy Snake arms (optional)	4- "Baladi," Raks Zahra
Glute contractions	5- "Bent elBald," Oriental Belly Dance vol. 2: Darbouka and Tabla

2. Standing Isolation Exercises & Dance Positions

Dance positions and body alignment	6- "The Sensual Chifti," Aziza Raks

Isolations in first, second and third dance positions:
    Glute contraction, hip lift
    Chest lift and drop
    Shoulder accent, roll and shimmy
	7- "Funk," Fate

Shimmy preparation and practice: focus on alignment and movement of the knees, relaxing the buttocks	8- "Shimmy," Belly Dance Music

1-2 minute break for water, questions, or comments

Winter Session
Week 1, continued

3. Movements for New Combinations

Isolations drill with baladi rhythm, incorporating: 　　Hip sway side to side 　　Hip lift 　　Belly pop 　　Chest lifts 　　Chest drops 　　Shoulder roll into shoulder shimmy	9- "Baladi"(7:27 version) Tribal Dance Tribal Drums
Practice movements at fast tempo	10- "Balady fast," Rhythm Identification

4. Culminating Activity: Isolations & Shimmy-optional Combinations

Students follow the teacher to perform isolations or drills to a short fun song. More experienced student may incorporate shimmy layering. **Assessment (optional):** Students perform the culminating activity without the teacher. Advanced students may lead.	11- "Hizzy Mazbout," Bellydance Superstars Vol. 5

5. Cool-down & Stretch

Perform fluid movements and do final stretches	12- "Nile Sunset," Sensual Art of Belly Dance: Slow Rhythms
	13- "Modern Mystics," Fire Dance

6. Thank and praise your students.

Promote a future class, community event, or say something about the topic of the next class. Wish them a wonderful evening, weekend or week.

Reflections:

What went well?

What could have been better?

Did the students' learning behaviors match your expectations?

What would you do differently next time?

Teaching Tip #13

Teach with confidence! Teaching with complete confidence and authority takes many hours of actual teaching. The more opportunities you take to hone your skills, the better your skills will get. However, it is simply not enough to acquire teaching hours. If you want to improve and learn on the job, you must reflect on and evaluate your own performance, and you must take student feedback into consideration.

Be a Role Model - You are a role model, whether you like it or not. Students look up to you, set a good example.

Be Authentic – Be true to your values and your teaching philosophy.

Teach without Ego – Continue to learn. Acknowledge your weaknesses but don't advertise them. Learn to laugh at yourself. If you believe in something, stick to it. Believe in yourself. And remember you can change your mind and correct yourself anytime you need.

Winter Session

Week 2
Horizontal Hip Figure 8 | Melodic Instruments | Chiftiftelli or Wahda rhythm

Teaching Objectives:

- Introduce students to horizontal hip figure 8's and variations
- Guide students in exploring the interpretation of the melodic instruments in Middle Eastern music, such as violin or accordion with horizontal hip figure 8
- Provide an opportunity for students to freely explore these movements in the context of the chiftitelli and wahda rhythms
- If appropriate, introduce students to the concept of taqsim, improvised instrumental solo

Isolations & Movements	Suggested Activity:	Dance positions:
• Hip slide • Hip twist **Horizontal movements** • Horizontal hip figure 8 • Weight shifted hip figure 8 and transition	Freestyle hip figure 8 practice to accordion or violin taqasim with chiftitelli, wahda kebira or wahda rhythm, focusing on the melody and rhythm separately, then both at once. Emphasize transition from weight-centered to weight-shifted movement. For challenge, use both horizontal and vertical hip figure 8's to explore these musical elements.	First position Second position

Procedure | Suggested Playlist

1. Introduction & Warm-up

Fast warm-up	1- "Sultana el Houb," Middle Eastern Dance: 30 Hits of Belly Dance
Slow warm-up	2- "Hatshepsut," Hatshepsut

Muscle Engagement Floor Exercises:
    Lower Abs/lower back
    Mid-Abs/mid-back
    Upper Abs/upper back (chest lift)
    Reverse order of contractions
	3- "Whisper," Amir Sofi: Amir

Ribcage twist Trapezius contraction Pectoral contraction Shoulder accents, roll and shimmy Snake arms (optional) Glute contractions	4- "Baladi," Raks Zahra
	5- "Bent elBald," Oriental Belly Dance vol. 2: Darbouka and Tabla

2. Standing Exercises & Movements

Dance positions, body alignment, weight shift transitions	6- "The Sensual Chifti," Aziza Raks
Lower abdominal contraction Hip slide Hip twist	7- "Tribal Dream," Bellydance Superstars Vol. 3
Shimmy preparation and practice: focus on alignment and movement of the knees, relaxing the buttocks	8- "Shimmy," Belly Dance Music

1-2 minute break for water, questions, or comments

Winter Session
Week 2, continued

3. Movements for New Combination/Activity

Horizontal hip figure 8, front to back
    Weight-centered
    Weight-shifted
    Weight-shift from side to side
	9- "Ana Fi Intizarak" (violin solo) Taqsim Lil Qamar

Horizontal hip figure 8, back to front
    Weight-centered
    Weight-shifted
    Weight-shift from side to side
	10- "El Amor Perdido," Flamenco Arabe

4. Culminating Activity: Horizontal Figure 8 Free-Style Practice

Students follow the teacher to perform in performing simple free-style figure 8 exploration.	11- "Houwa Sahih Al Hawa Ghallab," Raks Ayoub
Assessment (optional): Students perform the culminating activity without the teacher. Advanced students may lead.	

5. Final Activity

Review Isolations Drill from Week 1	12- "Hizzy Masbout," Bellydance Superstars Vol. 5

6. Cool-down & Stretch

Perform fluid movements and do final stretches	13 – "Nile Sunset," Sensual Art of Belly Dance: Slow Rhythms
	14- " Modern Mystics," Fire Dance

7. Thank and praise your students.

Promote a future class, community event, or say something about the topic of the next class. Wish them a wonderful evening, weekend or week.

Reflections:

What went well?

What could have been better?

Did the students' learning behaviors match your expectations?

What would you do differently next time?

Teaching Tip #14

Incorporate self-correction methodology from the very first class. Educate students on the position and alignment of their joints. Ask them to view or feel their form with specific criteria, so that they can begin to adjust into proper alignment on their own. This is a great strategy to avoid singling out students, as many people are extremely sensitive about this issue. Be patient. When you know your students better, you can determine the best correction techniques for different sensibilities.

Week 3
Vertical Hip Movements | Chiftitelli or Wahda Kebira & Baladi Rhythms| Transitions

Teaching Objectives:

- Begin preparing students for some of the more challenging movements and combinations of the choreography
- Introduce students to a common and useful technique for shifting weight and transitioning between movements

Key Isolations & Movements	Transitions Combination: Balady Rhythm (From "Zeina" choreography)	Dance Positions:
- Hip tilt - Glute contraction - Hip lift - Hip drop - Vertical hip figure 8 - Weight shifting hip figure 8 and transition with the feet	1) 2cts R hip drop (with glute contraction on L) 2) 4cts slow vertical hip figure 8 from L to R, completing the movement with weight on R. Repeat combination starting with L hip drop. **For added challenge:** 1) Mark the first two Doums of the baladi rhythm with hip drop (1AND). 2) Figure 8, on 3AND4. Repeat on other side.	Third position Foot positions for smooth transitions from R to L, and L to R.

Procedure | Suggested Playlist

1. Introduction & Warm-up

Procedure	Suggested Playlist
Fast warm-up	1- "Sultana el Houb," Middle Eastern Dance: 30 Hits of Belly Dance
Slow warm-up	2- "Hatshepsut," Hatshepsut

Muscle Engagement Floor Exercises:
    Lower Abs/lower back
    Mid-Abs/mid-back
    Upper Abs/upper back (chest lift)
    Reverse order of contractions
	3- "Whisper," Amir Sofi: Amir

Ribcage twist Trapezius contraction Pectoral contraction Shoulder accents, roll and shimmy Snake arms (optional)	4- "Baladi," Raks Zahra
Glute contractions	5- "Bent elBald," Oriental Belly Dance vol. 2: Darbouka and Tabla

2. Stationary Isolations & Movements

Procedure	Suggested Playlist
Dance positions, body alignment, weight shift transitions	6- "The Sensual Chifti," Aziza Raks
Hip slide Hip twist Hip tilt Glute contraction Hip lift Hip drop	7- "The Kings Consort," Sensual Art of Bellydance: Fast Rhythms

1-2 minute break for water, questions, or comments

3. Movements for New Combinations & Steps: Vertical Hip Articulation

Vertical hip figure 8	8- "El Amor Perdido," Flamenco Arabe
	9- "Chiftitelli Unplugged," Tribal Dance Tribal Drums, Vol. 2: Itneen
Hip drops with glute contraction on the first two "Doums" of baladi rhythm	10- "Balady slow" Rhythm Identification
	11- "Balady fast," Rhythm Identification

4. Culminating Activity: Hip Drop + Vertical Figure 8 Combination

Students follow the teacher to perform drills incorporating vertical hip figure 8 and hip drop. **Assessment (optional):** Students perform the culminating activity without the teacher. Advanced students may lead.	12-"Balady," The Dancing Drum

5. Final Activity

Leg shimmy preparation and practice	13- "Shimmy," Belly Dance Music

6. Cool-down & Stretch

Perform fluid movements and do final stretches	14- "Nile Sunset," Sensual Art of Belly Dance: Slow rhythms
	15- Modern Mystics," Fire Dance

7. Thank and praise your students.

Promote a future class, community event, or say something about the topic of the next class. Wish them a wonderful evening, weekend or week.

Reflections:

What went well?

What could have been better?

Did the students' learning behaviors match your expectations?

What would you do differently next time?

 Teaching Tip #15

If you would like to teach the art of finger cymbals to your students, introduce them in the first part of the class. Each week experienced students who are ready can begin playing simple patterns while practicing basic moves.

Week 4
Step-Touch, Two-Step | Baladi/Maqsoum & Ayoub Rhythms | Weight Change Dynamics

Teaching Objectives:

- Introduce students to two traveling steps that will be featured in the choreography
- Guide students in listening for, and stepping on the "doum"
- Provide an opportunity for students to use new steps to travel and use a large space

Key Isolations and Movements:	Across the Floor Practice:	Dance Positions & Transitions:
• Hip slide • Glute contraction • Hip lift • Hip twist **Steps & Traveling:** • Step-touch • Two-step	**Baladi or Maqsoum Rhythm** Step-touch fwd Step-touch back **Ayoub Rhythm** Two-step R foot lead Two-step L foot lead Experienced students may wish to add hip movements to the steps. Check alignment, knees and feet before encouraging the anticipated hip movements.	Third Position Fourth Position

Procedure | Suggested Playlist

1. Introduction & Warm-up

Fast warm-up	1- "Sultana el Houb," Middle Eastern Dance: 30 Hits of Belly Dance
Slow warm-up	2- "Hatshepsut," Hatshepsut

Muscle Engagement Floor Exercises:
    Lower Abs/lower back
    Mid-Abs/mid-back
    Upper Abs/upper back (chest lift)
    Reverse order of contractions
	3- "Whisper," Amir Sofi: Amir

Ribcage twist Trapezius contraction Pectoral contraction Shoulder accents, roll and shimmy Snake arms (optional)	4- "Baladi," Raks Zahra
Glute contractions	5- "Bent elBald," Oriental Belly Dance vol. 2: Darbouka and Tabla

2. Stationary Isolations & Movements

Body awareness, alignment & muscle engagement	6- "The Sensual Chifti," Aziza Raks
Horizontal hip figure 8 Hip lift Optional: Figure with chiftitelli rhythm	7- "Chiftitelli Unplugged," Tribal Dance Tribal Drums Vol. 2: Itneen
Hip drop with glute contraction Optional: Review hip drop + vertical figure 8 combination	8- "Balady slow," Rhythm Identification
	9- "Balady fast," Rhythm Identification

1-2 minute break for water, questions, or comments

Winter Session
Week 4, continued

3. New Movements & Steps: In-Place

Step-touch + hip lift	10- "Balady," The Dancing Drum OR "Maqsoum," Tribal Dance Tribal Drums
Two-step + hip twist + glute contraction R foot lead	11- "Ayoub Simple," Pulse of the Sphynx OR "Ayub slow," Rhythm Identification
L foot lead	12- "Ayoub Simple," Pulse of the Sphynx OR "Ayub slow," Rhythm Identification

4. Culminating Activity: Across the Floor Travel

Practice travel steps across the floor in fast tempo song in full time or half time as appropriate their experience and fitness level	13- "Ayoub," The Dancing Drum
	14- "Hizzy Mazbout," Bellydance Superstars Vol. 5
Assessment (optional): Students perform the culminating activity without the teacher. Advanced students may lead.	

5. Final Activity

Gentle shimmy practice	15- "Baladi," Arabic Rhythms

6. Cool-down & Stretch

Perform fluid movements and do final stretches	16- "Nile Sunset," Sensual Art of Belly Dance: Slow Rhythms
	17- "Modern Mystics," Fire Dance

7. Thank and praise your students.

Promote a future class, community event, or say something about the topic of the next class. Wish them a wonderful evening, weekend or week.

Reflections:

What went well?

What could have been better?

Did the students' learning behaviors match your expectations?

What would you do differently next time?

Teaching Tip #16

A few times a year, plan a special outing or field trip with your students. Road trip to a workshop, or go see a show. In between sessions is a great time to plan a get together. Feed students' hunger for information and expose them to many different aspects of the dance and culture to keep them motivated and inspired.

Week 5
Dynamic Traveling Combinations | Maqsoum/Baladi & Ayoub Rhythms | Direction Changes & Transitions

Teaching Objective:

- Guide students in conditioning the legs and feet to perform dynamic and demanding traveling steps
- Provide opportunity for students to practice direction changes and transitions in simple floor patterns
- Prepare students to perform two of the traveling combinations and transitions featured in the choreography

Key Isolations & Movements:	Suggested Combinations:	Dance Positions & Transitions:
- Glute contraction - Hip lift - Hip twist - Hip circle or **Dynamic Traveling** - Side-step (step-close-step) - Step-touch with hip lift - Two-step with hip twist	**Maqsoum or Baladi Rhythm** 2x Step-touch travel forward 3 steps to the side or diagonal fwd (8cts total) Repeat other direction. 2x Step-touch travel back 3 steps to the side or diagonal back (8 cts total) Repeat other direction. For challenge, add hip movements and pivots to steps. **Ayoub Rhythm** 8x Two-step R-L travel to R (16 cts) 8x Two-step L-R travel to L (16 cts) **For challenge:** - Add hip movements to the steps - Perform steps at different tempos, fulltime and double time	Third Position Fourth Position Direction Change

Procedure | Suggested Playlist

1. Introduction & Warm-up

Fast warm-up	1- "Sultana el Houb," Middle Eastern Dance: 30 Hits of Belly Dance
Slow warm-up	2- "Hatshepsut," Hatshepsut
Muscle Engagement Exercises: 　Lower Abs/lower back 　Mid-Abs/mid-back 　Upper Abs/upper back (chest lift) 　Reverse order of contractions	3- "Whisper," Amir Sofi: Amir
Ribcage twist Trapezius contraction Pectoral contraction Shoulder accents, roll and shimmy Snake arms (optional)	4- "Baladi," Raks Zahra
Glute contractions	5- "Bent elBald," Oriental Belly Dance vol. 2: Darbouka and Tabla

2. Stationary Isolations & Movements

Body awareness, alignment & muscle engagement	6- "The Sensual Chifti," Aziza Raks
Horizontal hip figure 8 Hip lift Optional: Figure 8 with chiftitelli rhythm	7- "Chiftitelli Unplugged," Tribal Dance Tribal Drums Vol. 2: Itneen
Hip drop with glute contraction Optional: Review hip drop + vertical figure 8 combination	8- "Balady slow," Rhythm Identification
	9- "Balady fast," Rhythm Identification

1-2 minute break for water, questions, or comments

Winter Session
Week 5, continued

3. New Combinations: Step-Hip + Three Steps/Two-Step Hip Twist

Step-touch hip lift + Three steps
 	
    Travel forward
 	
    Travel backward
	10- "Balady," The Dancing Drum OR "Maqsoum," Tribal Dance Tribal Drums

Two-step + hip twist + glute contraction
 	
    R foot lead travel R on a circular floor pattern
 	
    L foot lead travel L, in a circular floor pattern
	11- "Ayoub," The Dancing Drum

4. Culminating Activity: Across the Floor Travel

Students follow teacher in performing:
 	
    Two-step dynamic travel combination in circular floor patterns
 	
    Practice any other movements appropriate for the track
	12- "Shimmy," Belly Dance Music

Step-touch travel combination in a diagonal floor patterns Practice any other movements appropriate for the track **Assessment (optional):** Students perform the combinations without the teacher. Advanced students may lead.	13- "Snake Dance," Bal Anat This is a version of "Zeina." Instead of the ayoub section typically in this song, there is a slow taqasim section in the middle with chiftelli/wahda sonbati and ney,. This version is a good basic alternative of the song. You may wish to use only this version or in addition to the version recommended.

5. Cool-down & Stretch

Perform fluid movements and do final stretches	14- "Nile Sunset," Sensual Art of Belly Dance: Slow Rhythms
	15- "Modern Mystics," Fire Dance

6. Thank and praise your students.

Promote a future class, community event, or say something about the topic of the next class. Wish them a wonderful evening, weekend or week.

Reflections:

What went well?

What could have been better?

Did the students' learning behaviors match your expectations?

What would you do differently next time?

 Teaching Tip #17

Provide notes and handouts for students to review after class. In the old days, handouts were printed on paper and distributed in class. Today, with different technologies available to us, we can provide notes electronically. Notes do not need to be elaborate. A simple outline is enough to help students remember what was covered and to help them practice at home.

Week 6
Choreography, "Zeina" Part 1 | Khanun, Ney & Baladi Rhythm

Teaching Objectives:

- Introduce students to the choreography song with background information
- Prepare students for part 1 of the choreography, with emphasis on the first two or three combinations

Essential Technique Review:	*"Zeina" Breakdown: Part 1 Baladi	Suggested Steps:

• Third position Step-Touch
• Hip Lift
• Transitions/Directions
• Shoulder roll, accent and shimmy
• Rhythmic weight shift
	Intro: khanun intro, 16cts
	(1) :18 Vocals
	   4cts + 4 cts. Repeat
	(2) :28 Ney
	   8cts
	(3) :34 4cts x 4 cts Accents
	(4) :43 Orchestra
	   8cts + 4cts + 4 cts
	Repeat (1)
	Repeat (2)
	Repeat (3)
	Repeat (4)
		(1) Step-hip 2x, 3 steps to the side. Repeat to L
		(2) Weight shift half-time R, L, R, L (undulations will be added later)
		(3) R shoulder roll, shift to R, shoulder accents. Repeat to L. Repeat sequence.
		(4) R hip drop 2cts + figure 8 2cts. Repeat on L. **4-step + 3-step turn.
		**This part of combination has not been introduced. Pause or show only, then prepare to repeat 1, 2, 3 and 4.

Background Information:

"Zeina" is an Egyptian song composed by Mohamed Abdel Wahab one of the legendary composers from the Golden Era of Egyptian film and dance. The song is featured in the 1956 Egyptian film Zanouba, with dancer Samia Gamal, one of the most famous dancers of the time. "Zeina" is a must-have song in any belly dancer's repertoire.

*Version of "Zeina" used is from Bellydance Superstars, Volume 1.

1. Introduction & Warm-up

Fast warm-up	1- "Sultan el houb," Middle Eastern Dance: 30 Hits of Belly Dance
Slow warm-up	2- "Hatshepsut," Hashepsut

Warm-up Isolations
    Abdominal contraction
    Hip slide and twist
    Ribcage lift and slide
    Shoulder roll and accent
	3- "Whisper," Amir Sofi: Amir

Alignment: Review Isolations in different dance positions	4- "The Sensual Chifti," Aziza Raqs

2. Review & Practice of Key Movements for Part 1 of Choreography

Hip tilt Glute contraction	5- "Bent elbald," Oriental Belly Dance Vol. 2: Darbouka and Tabla
Hip lift Hip drop	6- "Shimmy," Belly Dance Music
Vertical hip figure 8	7- "Baladi," Raks Zahra

1-2 minute break for water, questions, or comments

3. Review Combinations for Choreography

(1) 2x Step-hip + 3 steps to the side (this will eventually become a 3-point turn). Repeat to L (2) 4x Weight shift half time, ie. R, L, R, L (undulations will be added later to this step)	8- "Balady," The Dancing Drum
(3) R shoulder roll, shift to R, shoulder accents. Repeat to L. Repeat sequence. (4) 2x R hip drop on 1AND + figure 8 2cts. Repeat on L. (Combination from week	9- "Maqsoum," Tribal Dance Tribal Drums

4. Culminating Activity: Part 1 of "Zeina" Choreography

Students follow the teacher to perform part 1 of the "Zeina" choreography; demonstrate and cue weight shifts only for movements and combinations that have not yet been introduced.	10 – "Snake Dance," Bal Anat
Assessment (optional): Students perform the choreography without the teacher. Advanced students may lead.	11- "Zeina," Bellydance Superstars Vol. 1

5. Cool-down & Stretch

Perform fluid movements and do final stretches	12 – "Nile Sunset," Sensual Art of Belly Dance: Slow Rhythms
	13- "Modern Mystics," Fire Dance

6. Thank and praise your students.

Remind students to sign up for the next session. Tell them a little about what you have planned. Wish them a wonderful evening, weekend or week.

Reflections:

How did the session go for you?

What did you learn about your students?

What would you do differently next time?

Teaching Tip #18

The goals and vision of your class should align with the business model or payment structure you offer. For example, if you teach a progressive format, offer your classes in sessions, rather than a class card drop-in format. If the individual classes in your program can be enjoyed as stand-alone classes, offer the class card drop-in format. If you do not have control over the registration format, create your classes to better fit the format that is offered. The key is to align these two things and avoid the frustrations of trying fit a square peg in a round hole.

Winter Session (Part 2)

Week 1 or 7
Undulations | Ney | Transitions & Weight Shifts

Teaching Objectives:

- Introduce students to the Ney, the Middle Eastern flute
- Introduce students to an essential movement in all styles of belly dance, the undulation, using sequential and coordinated muscle engagement
- Guide students in focusing on muscle-driven movements

Isolations and Accents:	Ney:	Dance Positions:
• Lower Abs/lower back • Mid-Abs/mid-back • Upper Abs/upper back • Trapezius contraction • Pectoral contraction • Should accents/shimmy • Chest lift **Articulations:** • Upper body undulation • Lower body undulation • Full body undulation **Steps: (Optional)** • Two-step (rock-step)	Practice freestyle weight-shifting undulations to the Ney, or similar instrument. Select music that inspires you. Share what you enjoy about performing undulations. Talk about the feeling, mood or texture of the music. If appropriate challenge, explore undulations with the two-step, contracting lower abdominals on the back step. *Encourage students to use their muscles, while keeping the lower back and knees relaxed.	First position Third position Weight change transition: • Half time R to L • Full time fwd to back, ie. two-step

Remember to check in with students frequently about where they "feel" the movement. Undulations are not typically painful on the back when performed correctly. In fact, undulations are a therapeutic and strengthening movement when performed correctly.

Procedure | Suggested Playlist

1. Introduction & Warm-up

Fast warm-up	1- "Arabiyon Ana" Bellydance Superstars Vol. 4
Slow warm-up	2- "Hatshepsut," Hatshepsut

Warm-up Isolations
    Lower Abdominal contraction
    Hip slide
    Gentle hip/pelvic circle
    Chest lift and drop
    Trapezius contraction
    Pectoral contraction
    Should accents/shimmy
	3- "Whisper," Amir Sofi: Amir

Alignment, dance positions & muscle engagement	4- "Bent el Shalabijah," Art of the BellyDance

2. Stationary Exercises: Muscle Engagement & Isolations

Chest slide fwd and back Mid-abdominal contraction Lower abdominal contraction Pelvic drop/release	5- "Balady," The Dancing Drum

1-2 minute break for water, questions, or comments

3. Introduce New Movements: Undulations

Upper body undulation	6- "Sword," Bal Anat
Lower body undulation	7- "Ocean Depth," Goddess Workout
Full body undulation (advanced students)	8- "Hatshepsut reprise," Hatshepsut

4. Culminating Activity: Undulations Free-Style Practice

Students follow the teacher to perform undulations in free style manner while following the melody and mood of selected music. **Assessment (optional):** Students perform the culminating activity without the teacher. Ask students where they "feel" the movement.	9- "Aazab (suffering), Secrets of the Eye

5. Final Activity (optional)

Review "Zeina" choreography, if appropriate, adding the undulations to appropriate section of music, depending on which version you are using.	10 - "Snake Dance," (Zeina) Bal Anat
	11- "Zeina," Bellydance Superstars, Vol. 5

6. Cool-down & Stretch

Review dance positions and do final stretches	12- "Nile Sunset," Sensual Art of Belly Dance
	13- "Modern Mystics," Fire Dance

7. Thank and praise your students

Promote a future class, community event, or say something about the topic of the next class. Wish them a wonderful evening, weekend or week, whichever is appropriate.

Reflections:

What went well?

What could have been better?

Did the students' learning behaviors match your expectations?

What would you do differently next time?

 Teaching Tip #19

When describing the relationship between lower and upper body, use the analogy of a tree. The legs and pelvis are the roots. The lower half of the torso is the trunk, and the arms and upper body are the leaves, branches, and flowers, that interact with natural elements. Musically, the lower body is the rhythm, and the upper body is the melody.

Winter Session (Part 2)

Week 2 or 8
Arm Frames, 3-Step Turn & Step Transition | Masmoudi Rhythm

Teaching Objectives:

- Introduce students to the concept of arm frames and movements that showcase the hip articulations of Oriental dance
- Guide students in the dynamics of weight shift to perform the 4-step and the 3-step turn
- Introduce students to the 8-count masmoudi kabir rhythm (two 'doums') and highlight the similar structure to the 4-count baladi/masmoudi saghir rhythm
- Prepare students to perform two combinations from "Zeina" choreography to the baladi rhythm

Key Articulations:	Combinations to Masmoudi Rhythm:	"Zeina" Choreography & Transitions, Part 1 with Arm Frames:
• Hip sway • Hip twist • Hip drop **Steps & Turns:** • Four-step • Three-step turn	Four-step (1, 2, 3, 4) Three-step turn (5, 6, 7, 8) Combination **(4)** from Zeina Choreography: R hip drop 2cts Figure 8 4cts Repeat on L Three-step (4cts) + Three-step turn Repeat sequence starting on L	(1) Step-hip 2x, 3 steps to the side. Repeat to L (2) Weight shift half-time R, L, R, L (undulations will be added later) (3) R shoulder roll, shift to R, shoulder accents. Repeat to L. Repeat sequence. (4) R hip drop 2cts + figure 8 2cts. Repeat on L **Transition:** 4-step + 3-step turn

Procedure | Suggested Playlist

1. Introduction & Warm-up

Fast warm-up	1- "Arabiyon Ana" Bellydance Superstars Vol. 4
Slow warm-up	2- "Hatshepsut," Hatshepsut

Warm-up Isolations:
    Abdominal contraction
    Hip slide or gentle circles
    Ribcage lift, twist
    Trapezius contraction
    Pectoral contraction
    Shoulder accent and roll
    Neck stretch and head circles
	3- "Whisper," Amir Sofi: Amir

Alignment and dance positions: Warm-up feet and legs	4- "Bent el Shalabijah," Art of the Bellydance by Voyager

2. Stationary Exercises: Muscle Engagement & Preparation for Arm Frames, Paths & Patterns

Practice isolations in the different dance positions accenting the "doums" of the masmoudi rhythm. Explore arm frames with a focus on form and smooth transitions:
    Glute contraction/hip sway
    Hip lift and drop
    Chest lift and slide
    Shoulder accents
	5- "Masmoudi Kabir," Egyptian Music & Appreciation for the Belly Dancer

Review combination (4) from "Zeina" at two tempos: Hip drop + vertical figure 8	6- "Masmoudi Kabir slow," Rhythm Identification 7- "Masmoudi Kebir," Pulse of the Sphynx

Winter Session (Part 2)
Week 2 or 8, continued

1-2 minute break for water, questions, or comment

3. New Combination: Four-Step with Three-Step Turn to Masmoudi

Four-step with arm movements at two tempos: step forward 1(R) 2(L) on the first two "Doums"; step back RL 3, 4 Repeat leading L	8- "Masmoudi Kabir slow," Rhythm Identification
	9- "Masmoudi Kebir," Pulse of the Sphynx
Four-step with three-step turn with arm transition at two tempos: turn on 5, 6, 7, hold 8	10- "Masmoudi Kabir slow," Rhythm Identification
	11- "Masmoudi Kebir," Pulse of the Sphynx
Combine the steps: step fwd 1(R) 2(L), step back 3(R) 4 (L); turn on next measure of baladi 1, 2, 3, hold 4. Review other "Zeina" combinations	12- "Balady," The Dancing Drum

4. Culminating Activity: Review "Zeina" Adding New Combination

Students follow the teacher to review the "Zeina" choreography adding the four-step with three-step turn transition	13- "Snake Dance," (Zeina) Bal Anat
Assessment (optional): Students perform the combinations without the teacher. Teacher may prompt. Advance students may lead.	14- "Zeina," Bellydance Superstars Vol. 1

5. Final Activity (optional)

Review two-step with hip twist in a short drill incorporating arm frames and transitions. Finish with standing hip shimmy.	15- "Shimmy," Belly Dance Music

6. Cool-down & Stretch

Review fluid movements and do final stretches.	16- "Nile Sunset," Sensual Art of Belly Dance: Slow Rhythms
	17- "Modern Mystics," Fire Dance

7. Thank and praise your students

Promote a future class, community event, or say something about the topic of the next class. Wish them a wonderful evening, weekend or week, whichever is appropriate.

Reflections:

What went well?

What could have been better?

Did the students' learning behaviors match your expectations?

What would you do differently next time?

Teaching Tip #20

Create a positive learning environment! In a positive learning environment, students feel valued, trusted, encouraged, listened to, noticed, and respected.

You are not responsible for the attitudes and sensibilities that students bring to the dance classroom, however, the manner in which you use verbal and body language conveys your class culture and values.

When you set the example that the dance space is a safe and supportive place, students will become contributors to that environment.

In order to maintain the wonderful learning environment that you have created, do not exemplify or tolerate behavior and language that results in students being judged, ignored, misunderstood, criticized, or their ideas rejected or stolen.

Winter Session (Part 2)

Week 3 or 9
Shimmies | Khanun Instrument | Wahda Rhythm

Teaching Objectives:

- Introduce students to the variations of the leg shimmy, a.k.a. the straight-leg shimmy
- Prepare students for a combination they will learn later in the choreography
- Continue to exposes students to the flavor of taqasim and other unique elements of Arabic music

Shimmies:	Khanun:	Dance positions & Body lines:

• Shoulder shimmies
• Leg shimmies
	Prepare or modify your favorite shimmy combinations for khanun
	
	OR
	
	Practice free style upper and lower body shimmies and variations, such as:
	
	   Weight-centered
	
	   Weight-shifted
	
	   Layered with arms or other elements
	
	Talk about what you think makes this moment in the music, the taqasim, special.
	
	Share how the khanun instrument makes you feel.
		First position
		
		Second position
		
		Third position
		
		Arm movements and transitions
		
		Expression and Freestyle Movement

Procedure | Suggested Playlist

1. Introduction & Warm-up

Fast warm-up	1- "Arabiyon Ana" Bellydance Superstars Vol. 4
Slow warm-up	2- "Hatshepsut," Hatshepsut

Sitting Warm-up Exercises
    Glute contraction
    Leg shimmy
    Ribcage lift, twist
    Trapezius contraction
    Pectoral contraction
    Shoulder accent, shimmy and roll
    Neck stretch and head circles
	3- "Batn Beats," Repercussion

Alignment and dance positions with a focus on awareness of the weight placement, hip and knee positions.	4- "Bent el Shalabijah," Art of the Bellydance by Voyager

2. Stationary Exercises: Preparation for Shimmies & Vibrations

Leg shimmy at slow and medium speeds	5- "Veiled Mystery," Sensual Art of Belly Dance: Slow Rhythms
Shoulder accent to shimmy at medium to fast speeds	6- "Full Moon Ritual," Goddess Workout

1-2 minute break for water, questions, or comments

3. Practice Shimmy Combinations & Free-Style Melodic Movement, ie. Taqasim

Lower body shimmy and vibrations
    Weight-centered dance positions
    Weight-shifted dance positions
	7- "Kanoun Mood," Jalilah's Raks Shari, Vol. 6: In a Beirut Mood

Upper and lower body shimmies
    Weight-centered dance positions
    Weight-shifted dance positions
	8- "Kanun Solo," Belly Dance Favorites- Live at Le Figaro

4. Culminating Activity: Review "Zeina" Choreography

Students follow the teacher to review the one or both versions of the "Zeina" choreography. **Assessment (optional):** Students perform the choreography without the teacher. Teacher may prompt. Advance students may lead.	9- "Zeina," Bellydance Superstars Vol. 1 (Part 1 only)
	10- "Snake Dance," (Zeina) Bal Anat

5. Cool-down & Stretch

Review fluid simple movements such as hip slide, horizontal figure 8, arms movements or undulations. Do final stretches.	11- "Nile Sunset," Sensual Art of Belly Dance: Slow Rhythms
	12- "Modern Mystics," Fire Dance

6. Thank and praise your students

Promote a future class, community event, or say something about the topic of the next class. Wish them a wonderful evening, weekend or week, whichever is appropriate.

Reflections:

What went well?

What could have been better?

Did the students' learning behaviors match your expectations?

What would you do differently next time?

Teaching Tip #21

There is a lot of discussion and blogging about whether Oriental dance should be taught through choreography or improvisation. All the great dancers know how to do both, while they may have a preference for one. You don't have to choose. Each requires different skill sets. You can (and should) expose students to both.

Winter Session (part 2)

Week 4 or 10

Two-Step with Hip Twist | "Zeina" Choreography Part 2, Ayoub Rhythm | Direction Change

Teaching Objectives:

- Help students refine traveling technique with hip articulation
- Introduce students to the circular and spiral floor patterns
- Introduce part 2 of "Zeina" choreography and Ayoub rhythm, providing relevant background information

Suggested Combination:	Ayoub Travel Drill:	"Zeina" Music Breakdown: Part 2 Ayoub
(1) Shimmy in place	Two-step hip twist and glute contraction travel R at half time, 8x (16cts). Repeat to L.	(1) 1:29, Ayoub Intro, 16 cts
(2) 2-Step hip twist R at half-time, 8x (16cts). Repeat to L.	Repeat combination at full speed if appropriate for the level of students.	(2) 1:38, 8cts + 8cts
(3) Figure 8 to R 2 cts. Shimmy 2cts. Repeat to L. Repeat sequence.	Variations with Transitions:	(3) 1:53, {2ct + 2 cts} x 4. Repeat.
Repeat (2)	8cts to R. Repeat to L.	Repeat (2)
Repeat (3)	4 cts to R. Repeat to L.	Repeat (3)
Repeat part 1.	2cts to R. Repeat to L.	Repeat part 1 Baladi.
Turn 2x, pose.	4cts Single hip-twist R L R L.	End pose.

Procedure | Suggested Playlist

1. Introduction & Warm-up

Fast warm-up	1- "Arabiyon Ana" Bellydance Superstars Vol. 4
Slow warm-up	2- "Hatshepsut," Hatshepsut

Warm-up Isolation
    Abdominal contraction
    Hip slide
    Ribcage lift, slide and twist
    Neck stretch and head circles
	3- "Whisper," Amir Sofi: Amir

Alignment and dance positions: Warm-up the legs and feet for dynamic traveling dynamics	

2. Stationary Exercises: Isolations, Movements & Steps

Hip twist Hip tilt Glute contraction Hip lift and drop	4- "Baladi," (7:27 version) Tribal Dance Tribal Drums
Horizontal hip figure 8s Vertical hip figure 8s	5- "Kings Consort," Sensual Art of Belly Dance: Fast Rhythms
Two-step with hip twist lead R	6- "Ayub slow," Rhythm Identification
Two-step with hip twist lead L	7- "Ayub slow," Rhythm Identification

1-2 minute break for water, questions, or comments

Winter (part 2)
Week 4 or 10, continued

3. Review Combinations for Part 2 of "Zeina" Choreography with Ayoub Rhythm

New ayoub combinations: Two-step hip twist travel on circle Horizontal hip figure 8 + leg shimmy	8- "Ayoub," The Dancing Drum
Review baladi combinations: Step-touch with hip lift + three step turn Hip drop with glute contraction + vertical hip figure 8	9- "Balady," The Dancing Drum

4. Culminating Activity: "Zeina" Choreography

Students follow the teacher to review the one or both versions of the "Zeina" choreography with a focus on the Ayoub section. **Assessment (optional):** Students perform the choreography without the teacher. Teacher may prompt. Advance students may lead.	10- "Zeina," Bellydance Superstars Vol. 1
	11- "Snake Dance," (Zeina) Bal Anat

5. Cool-down & Stretch

Review fluid simple movements such as hip slide, horizontal figure 8, arms movements or undulations. Do final stretches	12- "Modern Mystics," Fire Dance

6. Thank and praise your students

Promote a future class, community event, or say something about the topic of the next class. Wish them a wonderful evening, weekend or week, whichever is appropriate.

Reflections:

What went well?

What could have been better?

Did the students' learning behaviors match your expectations?

What would you do differently next time?

Teaching Tip #22

Use positive non-judgmental language. For example, refrain from negative body talk, even if it is about your own body. Remember, you are a role model. Instead, talk about how wonderfully diverse and unique our bodies are, with different shapes, sizes, colors and movement styles.

Week 5 or 11
Fast Footwork | Malfuf Rhythm | "Zeina" Choreography Practice | Floor Patterns

Teaching Objectives:

- Explore previously taught steps with a different rhythm
- Explore tempo changes and traveling floor patterns
- Review and refine technique, combinations and transitions of "Zeina" choreography

Steps:	2-Step Combination with Malfuf Rhythm	Floor Pattern:
Introduce relevé to help assist fast footwork **Dynamic & Fast Traveling:** 2-step hip twist (double time) a.k.a. choo-choo shimmy step **Arms & Body Carriage:** Practice strong lifted arms, arm frames and transitions.	For added challenge: Mark the "Doum" of the malfuf rhythm with a flat step, relevé on Tek Tek. 8x 2-Step-hip twist R full time (step R,L on Doum), 16 cts. Repeat to L. Repeat full time (step R on every Doum)	Take travel steps in a circular floor pattern to each side, creating a figure 8 floor pattern.

Procedure | Suggested Playlist

1. Introduction & Warm-up

Fast warm-up	1- "Arabiyon Ana" Bellydance Superstars Vol. 4
Slow warm-up	2- "Hatshepsut," Hatshepsut

Warm-up Isolations
    Abdominal contraction
    Hip slide
    Ribcage lift, slide, twist
    Shoulder accent, shimmy and roll
    Neck stretch and head circles
	3- "Whisper," Amir Sofi: Amir

Alignment and Dance Positions: Warm-up the legs and feet for dynamic traveling combinations	4- "Bent el Shalabijah," Art of the Bellydance by Voyager

2. Stationary Exercises: Isolations, Movements and Steps

Hip slide Hip tilt Horizontal hip figure 8 Vertical hip figure 8 down to up Review variations as time allows	5- "Baladi," (7:27 version) Tribal Dance Tribal Drums
Shimmy practice: Choose one or two types of shimmies for a relaxed drill	6- "Shimmy," Belly Dance Music

1-2 minute break for water, questions, or comments

Winter (part 2)
Week 5 or 11, continued

3. Review Two-Step Combinations for Malfuf Rhythm

Two-step hip twist Flat-ball variation	7- "Full Moon Ritual," Goddess Workout
Practice two-step combination with figure 8 floor pattern and arms paths	8- "Malfoof," The Dancing Drum
If time remains, add variation or introduce another simple combination or step for malfuf rhythm.	9- "Malfuf, the War," Wassan Pharaoun

4. Culminating Activity: Review "Zeina" Choreography

Students follow the teacher to review the one or both versions of the "Zeina" choreography.	10- "Zeina," Bellydance Superstars Vol. 1
Assessment (optional): Students perform the choreography without the teacher. Teacher may prompt. Advance students may lead.	11- "Snake Dance," (Zeina) Bal Anat

5. Cool-down & Stretch

Review dance positions and arm movement and do final stretches.	12- "Nile Sunset," Sensual Art of Belly Dance: Slow Rhythms
	13- "Modern Mystics," Fire Dance

6. Thank and praise your students

Promote a future class, community event, or say something about the topic of the next class. Wish them a wonderful evening, weekend or week, whichever is appropriate.

Reflections:

What went well?

What could have been better?

Did the students' learning behaviors match your expectations?

What would you do differently next time?

Teaching Tip #23

Encourage proper dress code by setting a good example. Some things to consider include:

Flooring – Is the surface good for turns? Is it clean? If the answer is "no" to either or both of these, you may need dance shoes.

Hip adornments - Do you find yourself yelling over the sound of a room full of jingly belts, or constantly stepping on belly dancer droppings? Perhaps fabric or sequin scarves will be less distracting and safer for class.

Tops and bottoms – Is your top too loose or baggy where students can't see what your joints and muscles are doing? Is your skirt to long or your pants too baggy that students can't see your knees? If so, you might consider investing in form fitting dance attire. Remember you don't have to bare your midriff, but students do need to be able to see your movements.

Hair – Does your hair get in the way of properly showing your form and movements? Long hair is great for performance, but it might be better to tie it up for class so that it does not distract or block the view of muscles and joints. If you're teaching "hairography" (dancing with hair tossing), then by all means, let it loose and go wild.

Winter Session (part 2)

Week 6 or 12
Review and Refine Movements & Choreography

Teaching Objectives:

- Lead students in performing the full choreography from start to finish
- Encourage students to ask questions and explore combinations freely
- Clarify and complete gaps in student understanding by checking for understanding

Review Complete Choreography:	**"Zeina" Breakdown: Part 1 Baladi**
Intro: khanun, 16cts	Intro: khanun, 16cts
(1) Step-hip 2x, 3 steps to the side. Repeat to L	**(1)** :18 Vocals 4cts + 4 cts. Repeat
(2) Weight shift half-time R, L, R, L (undulations will be added later)	**(2)** :28 Ney 8cts
(3) R shoulder roll, shift to R, shoulder accents. Repeat to L. Repeat sequence.	**(3)** :34 4cts x 4 cts Accents
(4) R hip drop 2cts + figure 8 2cts. Repeat on L. 4-step + 3-step turn. Repeat (1) Repeat (2) Repeat (3) Repeat (4)	**(4)** :43 Orchestra 8cts + 4cts + 4 cts Repeat (1) Repeat (2) Repeat (3) Repeat (4)
Part 2 Ayoub	**Part 2 Ayoub**
(1) Shimmy in place, 8cts x 2	**(1)** 1:29, Intro, 16 cts
(2) 2-Step hip twist R at half-time, 8x (16cts). Repeat to L.	**(2)** 1:38, 8cts + 8cts Repeat
(3) Figure to R 2 cts. Shimmy 2cts. Repeat 4x R to L. Repeat sequence. Repeat (2) Repeat (3) Repeat part 1 Baladi Turn 2x, pose	**(3)** 1:53, {2ct + 2 cts} x 4 Repeat. Repeat (2) Repeat (3) Repeat part 1 Baladi End

Procedure | Suggested Playlist

1. Introduction & Warm-up

Fast warm-up	1- "Arabiyon Ana" Bellydance Superstars Vol. 4
Slow warm-up	2- "Hatshepsut," Hatshepsut

Warm-up Isolations
    Abdominal contraction
    Hip slide
    Ribcage lift, slide, twist
    Shoulder accent, shimmy and roll
    Neck stretch and head circles
	3- "Whisper," Amir Sofi: Amir

Alignment and Dance Positions: Warm-up the legs and feet for dynamic traveling combinations	4- "Bent el Shalabijah," Art of the Bellydance by Voyager

2. Essential Review: Movements, Steps & Combinations

Abdominal Isolations Undulation	5- "El Amor Perdido," Flamenco Arabe
Glute contraction	6- "Bent elBald," Oriental Belly Dance Vol. 2: Darbouka and Tabla
Vertical hip figure 8	7- "Chiftitelli Unplugged" Tribal Dance Tribal Drums, Vol. 2: Itneen

1-2 minute break for water, questions, or comments

Winter Session (part 2)
Week 6 or 12, continued

4. Review Combinations

Step-hip and three-step turn	8- "Balady," The Dancing Drum
Four-step and three-step turn	
Undulations and shoulder roll or shimmy	
Hip drop and vertical figure 8	

4. Culminating Activity: Review & Perform "Zeina" Choreography

Students follow the teacher to review the one or both versions of the "Zeina" choreography.	9- "Zeina," Bellydance Superstars Vol. 1 (Part 1 only)
Assessment (optional): Split students into two groups. Each group performs the choreography for the others. You might consider the last class as a mini-hafla.	10- "Snake Dance," (Zeina) Bal Anat

5. Cool-down & Stretch

Review dance positions and fluid movements and do final stretches.	11- Modern Mystics," Fire Dance

6. Thank and praise your students

Promote a future class, community event, or say something about the topic of the next class. Wish them a wonderful evening, weekend or week, whichever is appropriate.

Reflections:

How did the session go for you?

What did you learn about your students?

What would you do differently next time?

Reminder!

Remember to get formal written feedback from your students. Make it easy for them to respond in a short simple written form or an easy online form. You may want to ask some of your returning students to submit a quote or testimonial for marketing purposes.

3

Spring Session:
Performance Skills

Pre-requisite for students: none

Learning Goals: Students become oriented to the parts of the stage and stage directions. It is expected that students will gain poise and self-confidence through the basics of stagecraft and showmanship. Students will become familiar stage formations along with the principals of presentation and/or props, such as veil. In addition students will be exposed to a variety of music and performance styles.

Technique	Music & Culture	Artistry
• Students will gain or improve body awareness and muscle control through the vocabulary of body isolations • Students will be able to perform strong poses, postures and movements through proper muscle engagement and body alignment • Students will become familiar with many traveling steps	• Students will be able to recognize the dynamics of music and rhythm progression in Oriental dance music • Students will explore the role of music in dance movements and use of the stage	• Students will be able to perform a sequence of choreographed drills or combinations in the performance styles presented • Students will practice poses and body lines of performance aesthetics • Students will gain an understanding of the many ways to use and "own" the stage

Grading Criteria: Rubrics for Student Evaluation (optional)

Objectives	Needs reinforcement	Solid understanding; benefits from practice	Mastery; enjoys advanced exploration
Improved body awareness and muscle control through the vocabulary of body isolations			
Perform strong poses, postures and movements through proper muscle engagement and body alignment			
Familiar with many traveling steps			
Recognize the dynamics of music and rhythm progression in Oriental dance music			
Effort in exploring the role of music in dance movements and use of the stage			
Perform a sequence of choreographed drills or combinations in the performance styles presented			
Confidence in practicing poses and body lines of performance aesthetics			
Understanding of the many ways to use and "own" the stage			

Spring Session (Part 1)

Week 1
Isolations | Masmoudi Kabir Rhythm | Dance Positions

Teaching Objectives:

- Engage students in body awareness through exercises for muscle isolation and body alignment of dance positions
- Create a simple combination that highlights or frames isolations and movements to introduce students to the concept of poses and stage presence
- Familiarize students with the concept of "Doum" and "Tek" in Arabic percussion, and the masmoudi kabir rhythm in particular, with three "Doums"

Lower Body Isolations:	**Note:** You may create a new combination or modify one from a previous lesson.	**Dance Positions:**
• Abdominal contraction		First position
• Abdominal release (belly pop)	**Isolations Drill Modified for Masmoudi Rhythm with 3 "Doums":**	
• Hip slide side-to-side	**Second Position/Arabesque pose** (weight on L)	Second position
• Glute contraction	Mark the accented beats of the masmoudi rhythm with body isolations:	
• Pelvic/hip tilt	Head slide	
Upper Body Isolations:	R shoulder accent	
• Chest lift (upper abs, upper back)	RLR shoulder accent	
• Chest drop	Chest drop	
• Chest slide (obliques, upper back, upper abs)	**Classic belly dance stance/Third Position**	Third position
• Trapezius contraction	Belly pop	
• Pectoral contraction	L glute contraction/R hip drop	
• Head slides (optional)	R glute contraction/L hip drop	
	Cross L over R to pivot (or shift L to R)	
	Repeat entire sequence 4x	

Procedure | Suggested Playlist

1. Introduction & Warm-up

Procedure	Suggested Playlist
Fast warm-up	1- "El Layali," Arabic Jukebox
Slow warm-up	2- "Aataba," Bellydance Superstars Vol. 4

Warm-up Isolations:
    Abdominal contraction
    Hip slide
    Ribcage lift, slide twist
    Shoulder roll back and forward
	3- "Lion Birds," Sensual Art of Belly Dance: Fast Rhythms

Body awareness, dance positions & muscle engagement	4- "Nai Solo," Ya Salam Ya Fahtiem

2. Stationary Exercises: Weight-Centered & Weight-Shifted Isolations & Movements

Isolations in first position: 　Abdominal contraction 　Abdominal release (belly pop) 　Hip slide side-to-side 　Hip tilt 　Glute contraction	5- "Maqsoum," Tribal Dance Tribal Drums
Isolations in second position: 　Chest lift 　Chest drop 　Chest slide 　Trapezius contraction 　Pectoral contraction 　Head slides and neck stretch	6- "DJ," Oriental Belly Dance Vol. 2: Darbouka and Tabla
Isolations in third position: 　Hip lift 　Hip drop 　Glute contraction	

1-2 minute break for water, questions, or comments

Spring Session
Week 1, continued

3. New Movements: Practice Combinations for Isolations Drill

Second Position (Arabesque) (weight on L) Mark the first 3 beats of the Masmoudi rhythm with body isolations:
 	
    Head slide
    R shoulder accent
    RLR shoulder accent
    Chest drop
	7- "Masmoudi Kebir," Drum Rhythms for Oriental Dance with Mohammed "Bibo" Gaber

Third Position (Classic belly dance)
 	
    Belly pop
    L glute contraction/R hip drop
    R glute contraction/L hip drop
    Cross L over R to pivot (or shift L to R)
	8- "Masmoudi," The Dancing Drum Vol. 1

4. Culminating Activity: Isolations Drills with Masmoudi Rhythm

Students follow the teacher to perform isolations in dance positions that highlight the movements, with emphasis on form and alignment along with smooth transitions from one position to the next.	9- "Kebrieaa Samet," Flamenco Arabe
Assessment (optional): Students perform the drill sequence without the teacher. Teacher may prompt. Advance students may lead.	

5. Cool-down & Stretch

| Perform fluid movements and do final stretches. | 10- "Desert Twilight," Fire Dance |

6. Thank and praise your students.

Promote a future class, community event, or say something about the topic of the next class. Wish them a wonderful evening, weekend or week.

Reflections:

What went well?

What could have been better?

Did the students' learning behaviors match your expectations?

What would you do differently next time?

Teaching Tip #24

Performing movements only on one side of the body creates muscles imbalances and can cause overuse injuries. Be sure to introduce and practice all movements on both sides of the body. Practice combinations and steps starting on both the right and the left, as well as turns to both directions.

Week 2

Horizontal Hip Circle, Hip Figure 8, Chest Circle | Wahda Rhythm & Musical Phrasing | Weight Shift Awareness & Transitions

Teaching Objectives:

- Introduce students to horizontal movements, such as hip circle, figure 8 and ribcage circle
- Help students gain better muscle control and flexibility for proper alignment
- Guide students to identify the "Doum" of the wahda rhythm
- Begin preparing students for transitions and directional changes

Key Isolations & Movements	Suggested Combinations to Wahda Rhythm	Dance Positions:
• Hip slide fwd/back • Hip slide side/side • Hip twist • Horizontal hip circle • Horizontal hip figure 8 (one or both directions) • Ribcage slide fwd/back • Ribcage slide side/side • Horizontal ribcage circle	**Combination 1:** **Hip circle to R** (clockwise) 4x, or 4 measures (start each circle on the L and shift to R with the "Doum," end on R) **Chest circle to R** at (clockwise) 4x, or 4 measures Repeat to hip circles to L. End on L. Repeat chest circles to L. Repeat sequence 4x or more. **Hip Figure 8** Begin each figure 8 on the "Doum." One figure 8 = one measure of wahda rhythm. For added challenge, explore weight shifts, tempo changes, and directional pivot during weight shifts.	Third position Arm poses and frames

Procedure | Suggested Playlist

1. Introduction & Warm-up

Fast warm-up	1- "El Layali," Arabic Jukebox
Slow warm-up	2-"Aataba," Bellydance Superstars Vol.4

Warm-up Isolations:
    Abdominal contraction
    Hip slide
    Ribcage lift, slide and twist
    Shoulder roll back and forward
	3- "Lion Birds," Sensual Art of Belly Dance: Fast Rhythms

Body awareness, dance positions & muscle engagement	4- "Nai Solo," Ya Salam Ya Fahtiem

2. Stationary Exercises: Review & Practice Key Isolations & Movements

Isolations in first position:
    Abdominal contraction
    Abdominal release (belly pop)
    Hip slide side-to-side
    Hip tilt
    Glute contraction
	5- "Maqsoum," Tribal Dance Tribal Drums

Isolations in second position:
    Chest lift
    Chest drop
    Chest slide
    Trapezius contraction
    Pectoral contraction
    Head slides and neck stretch	

Isolations in third position:
    Hip lift
    Hip drop
    Glute contraction	

Review Isolations Drill from week 1	6- "Masmoudi Kebir," Drum Rhythms for Oriental Dance with Mohammed "Bibo" Gaber

1-2 minute break for water, questions, or comments

3. Review & Practice of Key Movements: Find the "Doum"

Hip slide fwd/back Hip slide to side Hip twist	7- "Wahda Sogaraya (Base and Variations [feat. Khamis Henkesh]" Rhythms of Oriental Dance
Horizontal hip circle Horizontal hip figure 8	

4. Movements for New Combinations & Steps with Wahda Rhythm

Horizontal hip circle Ribcage circle	8- "Tawil or Wahda Clasical Rhythm," Arab Rhythmology
Horizontal hip figure 8	9- "Sunrise over Giza," Sensual Art of Belly Dance: Slow Rhythms

5. Culminating Activity: Isolations Drill with Wahda Rhythm

Students follow the teacher to perform the suggested combinations with horizontal hip and ribcage circle, and the horizontal hip figure 8, beginning each movement or transition on the "doum" of each measure. **Assessment (optional):** Students perform the combination without the teacher. Teacher may prompt. Advance students may lead.	10- "El Amor Perdido," Flamenco Arabe

Spring Session
Week 2, continued

6. Cool-down & Stretch

Review dance positions, perform fluid arm movements and do final stretches	11- "Desert Twilight," Fire Dance

7. Thank and praise your students.

Promote a future class, community event, or say something about the topic of the next class. Wish them a wonderful evening, weekend or week.

Reflections:

What went well?

What could have been better?

Did the students' learning behaviors match your expectations?

What would you do differently next time?

Teaching Tip #25

When teaching performance concepts, emphasize that the purpose is fun and to build confidence before actually performing for an audience. Encourage those who are interested in performing to continue with classes, put forth their best effort and follow up at home with extra practice. Make a distinction between professional performance venues and environments more suitable for students.

Week 3

Hip Lift, Hip Drop, Vertical Hip Figure 8| Baladi/Maqsoum | Step Transition | Direction Changes

Teaching Objectives:

- Prepare students for travelling, turns and using the stage by introducing direction changes and weight transitions
- Guide students in a simple combination with vertical hip movements hip lift and hip drop that incorporate a step transition

Isolations & Articulations	Suggested Combinations	Dance Positions:
• Hip slide • Glute contraction • Hip tilt • Hip lift • Hip drop • Hip twist **Weight Shift:** • Step • Touch • Transition: push off the ball of the foot	**Combination 1:** 2 x Step-hip lift (4 cts) Step-touch hip lift front, side, back, ie. fourth, second, and fifth positions, respectively (4 cts) 8 cts total. Repeat other side. For added challenge: Pivot with each step to the diagonal (DS hip is active) Travel with the step forward, back or pivot 360 degrees. **Combination 2 or Alternate Version of Combo 1:** 2x Step-touch hip lift (4cts) Step-hip drop 3x 8cts total. Repeat other side. For added challenge, travel forward then back. **Combination 3:** Start R, vertical hip figure 8, push off the ball of the foot to L 4cts Hip drop on R 4cts Repeat start L.	Second position Fourth Position Fifth Position

Spring Session
Week 3, continued

Procedure | Suggested Playlist

1. Introduction & Warm-up

Fast warm-up	1- "El Layali," Arabic Jukebox
Slow warm-up	2- "Aataba," Bellydance Superstars Vol. 4

Warm-up Isolations:
    Abdominal contraction
    Hip slide
    Ribcage lift, slide and twist
    Shoulder roll back and forward
	3- "Lion Birds," Sensual Art of Belly Dance: Fast Rhythms

Body awareness, dance Positions & muscle engagement	4- "Nai Solo," Ya Salam Ya Fahtiem

2. Stationary Exercises: Weight-Shifted Isolations & Movements

Isolations in first position:
    Hip slide
    Hip tilt
	5- "Maqsoum," Tribal Dance Tribal Drums

Isolations in second position:
    Glute contraction
    Hip lift	

Isolations in third position:
    Glute contraction
    Hip twist	

Optional: Review combinations from week 2
    Horizontal hip and ribcage circle
    Horizontal hip figure 8
	6- "Amor Perdido," Flamenco Arabe

1-2 minute break for water, questions, or comments

3. Review & Practice of Key Movements: Hip Lift, Hip Drop, Dynamics of Basic Transitions & Weight Shifts

Hip lift Hip drop	7- "Baladi," (7:29 version) Tribal Dance Tribal Drums
Difference between a step and touch: Practice Step-touch transition between a series of hip lifts and drops Other transition: Shift weight by push off the ball of the foot	

4. Movements for New Steps: Hip Lift & Vertical Hip Figure 8 Combination

Vertical hip figure 8	8- "Streams on the Nile," Ahla Leila
Vertical hip figure + hip drop	

5. Culminating Activity: Practice Vertical Movement Combinations

Students follow the teacher to perform the step-touch hip lift and drop combinations, alternating with vertical hip figure 8 combination. Review horizontal movement combination from week 2 when the rhythm changes to wahda.	9- "Awal Suhur," Musica Arabe Instrumental Vol. 7
Assessment (optional): Students perform the combinations without the teacher. Teacher may prompt. Advance students may lead.	

Spring Session
Week 3, continued

6. Final Activity: Shimmy Preparation & Practice

Practice the motion of legs, engaging in the abdominals and obliques.	10- "Eshta," Raks Zahra

7. Cool-down & Stretch

Perform fluid movements and do final stretches	11- "Desert Twilight," Fire Dance

8. Thank and praise your students.

Promote a future class, community event, or say something about the topic of the next class. Wish them a wonderful evening, weekend or week.

Reflections:

What went well?

What could have been better?

Did the students' learning behaviors match your expectations?

What would you do differently next time?

Teaching Tip #26

Before sending students off to explore a large space, be sure to set the guidelines and ground rules. They will need to know direction of travel, when and where to start and end, and how to interact as a group. Be specific and demonstrate. Be patient if some students don't get it right away. They will get better with practice and repeated explanation.

Week 4

Step-Touch, Arabesque Walk, Side-Step | Orchestra, Rhythm & Melody | Introduction to Floor Patterns

Teaching Objectives:

- Prepare students to perform traveling steps with exercises to learn the foot and arm positions associated with steps
- Create a combination to begin orienting students to stage directions: Stage Center, Stage R, Stage L, Downstage and Upstage
- Introduce students to musical flavors and sounds that propel traveling, use of space and large movements

Steps & Traveling	Traveling Stage Pattern to Orchestral Melody:	Stage Positions:
• Step-touch • Step-pivot • Arabesque walk (step 1, 2, 3 hold, touch or pivot on 4) • Side-step (step-close-step)	Each dancer starts at upstage center (USC) Travel DS leading R. Travel SR leading R to offstage. Repeat to L starting again at USC **Travelling Pattern with the Step-Combinations** **Combination 1:** Starting at SC, step-hip travel fwd DS leading R. At SC change to side-step traveling SR. Repeat leading L. **Combination 2:** Arabesque walk fwd DS leading R. Continue Arabesque walk to SR in crescent pattern. Repeat leading L.	DS = Down Stage, closest to the audience US = Upstage, furthest from the audience SR = Stage Right, dancer's right when facing the audience SL = Stage Left, dancer's left when facing the audience SC = Stage Center, center of the stage **Floor Patterns:** Modified "Soul Train" formation • Travel DS • Travel SR or SL circling back to USC

Spring Session
Week 4, continued

Procedure | Suggested Playlist

1. Introduction & Warm-up

Fast warm-up	1- "El Layali," Arabic Jukebox
Slow warm-up	2- "Aataba," Bellydance Superstars Vol. 4

Warm-up Isolations:
  Abdominal contraction
 	
  Hip slide
 	
  Ribcage lift, slide and twist
 	
  Shoulder roll back and forward
	3- "Lion Birds," Sensual Art of Belly Dance: Fast Rhythms

Body awareness, dance positions & muscle engagement	4- "Nai Solo," Ya Salam Ya Fahtiem

2. Stationary Exercises: Weight-Shifted Isolations & Movements

Isolations in first position:
  Hip slide
 	
  Hip tilt
	5- "Maqsoum," Tribal Dance Tribal Drums

Isolations in second position:
  Glute contraction
 	
  Hip lift	

Isolations in third position:
  Glute contraction
 	
  Hip twist	

1-2 minute break for water, questions, or comments

3. Review & Practice of Key Movements

Review one or more movements or combinations from weeks 2 and 3	6- "Awal Suhur," Musica Arabe Instrumental Vol. 7

4. Movement for New Steps & Combinations: Step-Touch, Step-Close-Step, Arabesque Walk & Pivot

Across the Floor: 　Step-touch 　Step-pivot 　Arabesque walk (step 1, 2, 3 hold, touch or pivot on 4)	7- "Baladi," (7:29 version) Tribal Dance Tribal Drums
Side-step (step-close-step): Add movements as desired	

5. Culminating Activity: Traveling the Stage

Review and practice each step by traveling the stage in the "Soul Train" style pattern	8- "Ahla Leila," Ahla Leila
Students follow the teacher to perform the combinations, traveling a single file line starting at upstage center, in a modified "Soul Train" style floor pattern. **Assessment (optional):** Students perform the steps and formations without the teacher. Advanced students may take turns leading.	

**Spring Session
Week 4, continued**

5. Cool-down & Stretch

| Perform fluid movements, review dance positions and do final stretches. | 9- "Desert Twilight," Fire Dance |

6. Thank and praise your students.

Promote a future class, community event, or say something about the topic of the next class. Wish them a wonderful evening, weekend or week.

Reflections:

What went well?

What could have been better?

Did the students' learning behaviors match your expectations?

What would you do differently next time?

Teaching Tip #27

Arm movements are big and noticeable and a great way to visually cue changes in movements and directions when the phrase changes. When changing direction or movements, cue the change two beats before the new phrase by extending or moving the arm on the active side or direction of travel.

Week 5

Three-Step Chassé, Three-Step Turn | Malfuf & Wahda Rhythms | Introduction to Group Formations

Teaching Objectives:

- Create a simple combination for students to practice traveling steps and floor patterns
- Engage students in listening for and stepping on the "Doum" in wahda and malfuf rhythms

Key Isolations & Movements:	Dynamic Step Combinations:	Dance Positions:
- Hip slide - Glute contraction - Hip sway - Ribcage tilt **Steps:** - Arabesque walk - Three-step chassé - Three-step turn - Tip-toe turn	**Combination 1: In Place Malfuf Rhythm** Three-step chasse side-to-side 12cts (6x) Three walking steps with hip sway, 4cts 16cts Repeat other side. Repeat sequence, replace hip sways with Three-step turn **Combination 2: Group Circle Traveling CW Wahda Rhythm** R Three-step chasse 12cts (6x) Three-step turn to R Repeat on L **Combination 3: Group Circle** R Three-step chasse 8ctx (4x) Three-step turn to R Tip-toe turn to L in place 16cts Repeat on L	Second position Fourth position **Group Circle: Expand & Contract:** Turn to R, toward the center of the circle, contract the circle Turn to L, away from the center of the circle, expand the circle

Procedure | Suggested Playlist

1. Introduction & Warm-up

Fast warm-up	1- "El Layali," Arabic Jukebox
Slow warm-up	2- "Aataba," Bellydance Superstars Vol. 4

Warm-up Isolations:
    Abdominal contraction
    Hip slide
    Ribcage lift, slide and twist
    Shoulder roll back and forward
	3- "Lion Birds," Sensual Art of Belly Dance: Fast Rhythms

Body awareness, dance positions & muscle engagement	4- "Nai Solo," Ya Salam Ya Fahtiem

2. Stationary Exercises: Find the "Doum"

Hip slide	5- "Waheda slow," Rhythm Identification
Hip tilt Glute contraction	6- "Wahed fast," Rhythm Identification
Hip sway (glute contraction with weight shift) 3-step hip sway (double side to side hip sway)	7- "Tawil or Wahda Clasical Rhythm," Arab Rhythmology
Tip-toe turn Three-step turn	8- "Wahda Sogaraya (Base and Variation) [feat. Khamis Henkesh]

1-2 minute break for water, questions, or comments

3. Review & Practice of Key Movements: Three-Step & Three-Step Turn

Three-step with Turns (In place): Three-step with hip sway Three walking steps with hip sway Replace hip sways with three-step turn Replace three-step turn with tip-toe turn	9- "Veiled Mystery," Sensual Art of Belly Dance: Slow Rhythms

4. New Steps & Concepts for Combinations: Arabesque, Three-Step Chassé

Across the Floor: Arabesque walk (preparation for chassé	10- "Leff slow," Rhythm Identification
Three-step chassé	11- "MALFUF lento," Todos los Ritmos Arabes
Three-step chassé with hip sway	12- "Malfouf Egyptian Rhythm," Arab Rhythmology

5. Culminating Activities: Group Formation & Use of the Stage

Practice each step in group circle R Three-step chasse 12cts (6x) Three-step turn to R Repeat on L	13- "Malfuf (Part 1)" Afrika Percussion Journey, Vol. 1
Students follow the teacher to perform the combination, traveling a single file line starting at upstage center, in a modified "Soul Train" style floor pattern.	14- "Arabian Gypsy," Dreaming the Diaspora
Assessment (optional): Students perform the steps and formations without the teacher. Advanced students may take turns leading.	

Spring Session
Week 5, continued

6. Cool-down & Stretch

Perform fluid movements and do final stretches	15- "Desert Twilight," Fire Dance

7. Thank and praise your students.

Promote a future class, community event, or say something about the topic of the next class. Wish them a wonderful evening, weekend or week.

Reflections:

What went well?

What could have been better?

Did the students' learning behaviors match your expectations?

What would you do differently next time?

Teaching Tip #28

Look for inexpensive silk veils to buy in bulk as loaners for class use. New students should never be forced to purchase props that are not an essential part of your curriculum. If you wish for students to purchase their own veils or other materials, the information needs to be conveyed in the class description, before the student registers. Students should be able to easily find out what materials are required before they step foot in your class. This information should be prominently posted at the registration location, whether it is online, in a flyer, or in person at the studio.

Week 6

Introduction Veil Dancing | Ney, Violin| Stage Dynamics of Veil

Teaching Objectives:

- Introduce students to basic veil technique
- Guide students to improve posture, arm carriage and upper body flexibility
- Lead students in fun combinations that will help them feel graceful and confident

Key Isolations & Movements:	Veil Maneuvers, Musicality and Context:	Dance Aesthetics:
• Abdominal contraction • Ribcage vertical circle • Ribcage figure 8 (dynamic) • Hip figure 8 (any version) • Shoulder rolls and arm circles • Wrist/forearm rotation • Hand position and veil grip **Steps:** • Arabesque Walk • Three-step chassé • Three-step turn • Four-step walking turn	Choose 2 or 3 of your favorite veil frames that highlight body movements, such as ribcage circle and hip figure 8s, with appropriate music for veil dancing Choose up to 4 of your favorite veil maneuvers, simplified for new beginners, to sophisticated for more experienced students Practice veil frames and maneuvers in "follow the teacher" format or create a few simple combinations to drill.	Stage formations, "Soul Train" style group veil dance Emphasize core engagement, relaxed shoulders and strong lifted upper back. Encourage exploration, experimentation and personal expression.

Spring Session
Week 6, continued

Procedure | Suggested Playlist

1. Introduction & Warm-up

Fast warm-up	1- "El Layali," Arabic Jukebox
Slow warm-up	2- "Aataba," Bellydance Superstars Vol. 4

Warm-up Isolations:
    Abdominal contraction
    Hip slide
    Ribcage lift, slide and twist
    Shoulder roll back and forward
	3- "Lion Birds," Sensual Art of Belly Dance: Fast Rhythms

Body awareness, dance positions & muscle engagement	4- "Nai Solo," Ya Salam Ya Fahtiem

2. Stationary Exercises: Review of Key Isolations & Movements

Review Isolations Drill from week 1	5- "Kebrieaa Samet," Flamenco Arabe
Choose two or three combinations from week 2 and 3 to review	6- "Awal Suhur," Musca Arabe Instrumental Vol. 7

1-2 minute break for water, questions, or comments

3. Introduction to Veil Maneuvers

Basic veil concepts
    How to hold the veil
    Posture and alignment during maneuvers
    Simple veil twirl/circle
    Favorite veil frames for basic movements
	7- "Whispers of Rumi," Goddess Workout

Favorite veil combinations:	8- "Ana Wehabibi," Rough Guide to Belly Dance (First Edition)

4. Culminating Activity: Group Formation & Use of the Stage

Students perform veil combinations in a stage formation, starting from upstage center in "Soul Train" style two-by-two, following the teacher's lead. **Assessment (optional):** Students perform veil combinations one at a time in the stage formation.	9- "Arabian Gypsy," Dreaming the Diaspora

Spring Session
Week 6, continued

5. Cool-down & Stretch

| Perform fluid movements and do final stretches | 10- "Desert Twilight," Fire Dance |

6. Thank and praise your students.

Promote a future class, community event, or say something about the topic of the next class. Wish them a wonderful evening, weekend or week.

Reflections:

What went well?

What could have been better?

Did the students' learning behaviors match your expectations?

What would you do differently next time?

Teaching Tip #29

It is common for students to overuse the shoulders in veil work. Teaching movement from the core will help keep the strain on the shoulders to a minimum. Be sure to instruct students to keep the shoulders down and relaxed when lifting the arms and maneuvering the veil, and to initiate movements from the core.

Spring Session (Part 2)

Week 1 or 7

Undulations | Baladi/Maqsoum Rhythm| Dance Positions

Teaching Objectives:

- Engage students in body awareness through conditioning exercises that prepare the muscles for internal movements
- Introduce students to the concept sequential movement of body undulations
- Emphasize the importance of muscle engagement in dance safety, aesthetics and enjoyment

Isolation Exercises:	Practice Undulations to Baladi/Maqsoum Rhythm:	Dance Positions:
• Lower Abs/lower back (pelvic floor) • Mid-Abs/mid-back • Upper Abs/upper back • Glute contraction • Trapezius isolation • Pectoral isolation • Shoulder accents/shimmy • Chest lift **Articulations:** • Upper body undulation • Lower body undulation • Full body undulation (optional)	**Lower body undulation** Accent each "Doum" with abdominal contraction stage of undulation **Upper and/or Full Body Undulation** Accent chest up/lift on first "Doum" and down on the second "Doum", ie. counts 1 and 3 Add a weight shift between each undulation	First position Third position

Spring Session (Part 2)
Week 1 or 7, continued

Procedure | Suggested Playlist

1. Introduction & Warm-up

Fast warm-up	1- "Walk Like an Egyptian," Bellydance Superstars, Vol. 2
Slow warm-up	2- "Aataba," Bellydance Superstars Vol. 4

Warm-up Isolations: Locate the muscles
    Lower abs and lower back
    Middle abs and middle-back
    Upper abs and upper back
	3- "Lion Birds," Sensual Art of Belly Dance: Fast Rhythms

Body awareness, dance positions & muscle engagement	4- "Nai Solo," Ya Salam Ya Fahtiem

2. Stationary Exercises: Muscle Engagement & Isolations

Hip slide	5- Maksoum," Arabic Rhythms
Hip tilt	6- "Bring it Down," The SharQui Workout
Glute contraction	7- "Baladi Seghir," Hatshepsut

Contract and Release Exercises:
    Lower abdominals/lower back
    Middle abdominals/mid-back
    Upper abdominals/upper back
    Chest lift
    Trapezius contraction
    Pectoral contraction
    Should accent/shimmy
	8- "Kings Consort," Sensual Art of Belly Dance: Fast Rhythms

1-2 minute break for water, questions, or comments

3. New Movements: Undulations

Upper body undulation	9-"Dance Dolphin Dance," Goddess Workout
Lower body undulation	
Full body undulation (optional)	10- "Streams on the Nile," Ahla Leila

4. Culminating Activity: Undulations Practice & Exploration

| Students follow the teacher to perform variety of undulations in different dance positions | 11- "Tribal Dream," Belly Dance Superstars, Vol. 3 |
| **Assessment (optional):** Students perform the undulations without the teacher. | |

5. Final Activity (optional)

| Short shimmy or hip drill | 12- "Urban Bedu," Repercussion |

6. Cool-down & Stretch

| Perform fluid movements, review dance positions and do final stretches. | 13- "Desert Twilight," Fire Dance |

7. Thank and praise your students

Promote a future class, community event, or say something about the topic of the next class. Wish them a wonderful evening, weekend or week, whichever is appropriate.

Reflections:

What went well?

What could have been better?

Did the students' learning behaviors match your expectations?

What would you do differently next time?

Reminder!

Guide students to self-correction or walk the room to offer feedback and correction discreetly. Whatever your style of correction, be sure it is positive, respectful and encouraging.

Week 2 or 8

4/4 (or 3/4) Hip Shimmy| Upper Body Shimmy | Rhythm & Melody | Body Lines & Dance Positions

Teaching Objectives:

- Engage students in driving dynamic shimmy technique from the obliques
- Prepare students to begin layering shimmies with other movements and traveling steps
- Introduce students to the concept of poses and body alignment to highlight different modes or flavors of shimmies
- Demonstrate and guide students performing shimmies to highlight both the rhythmic and melodic elements of traditional, modern and alternative belly dance music.

Key Isolations & Movements	Rhythm & Melody with Shimmies:	Dance Positions & Body Lines:
• Lower and upper abdominal contraction • Trapezius and pectoral contraction • Ribcage twist • Hip tilt • Lower body undulation • 4/4 hip shimmy • 3/4 hip shimmy • Shoulder or chest shimmy	Practice 4/4 and 3/4 hip shimmy and shoulder shimmies to any music with a steady beat and a melody. Combine shimmies and undulation in a simple steady free-style format to a high-energy song with full orchestra or other rich sound.	Second position, emphasizing introspection First position or half time walk with elegant arms, emphasizing playfulness

Spring Session (Part 2)
Week 2 or 8, continued

Procedure | Suggested Playlist

1. Introduction & Warm-up

Fast warm-up	1- "Walk Like an Egyptian," Bellydance Superstars, Vol. 2
Slow warm-up	2- "Aataba," Bellydance Superstars Vol. 4

Warm-up Isolations:
    Abdominal contraction
    Chest lift, slide, twist
	3- "Lion Birds," Sensual Art of Belly Dance: Fast Rhythms

Body awareness, dance positions & muscle engagement	4- "Nai Solo," Ya Salam Ya Fahtiem

2. Stationary Exercises: Muscle Engagement & Isolations

Hip slide	5- Maksoum," Arabic Rhythms
Hip tilt	6- "Bring it Down," The SharQui Workout
Glute contraction	7- "Baladi Seghir," Hatshepsut
Shimmy preparation: Practice the motion of the knees, relaxing the legs and buttocks	8- "Baladi," Arabic Rhythms

1-2 minute break for water, questions, or comments

3. Introduce Movements for Shimmies

Weight-centered shimmies
 	
Shimmies in different dance positions:
 	
    Hip shimmy half time, full time, double time
 	
    Shoulder Shimmy
	9- "Batn Beats," Repercussion

Review undulations	10-"Tribal Dream," Belly Dance Superstars, Vol. 3

4. Culminating Activity: Shimmy & Undulations Practice

Students follow the teacher to perform simple free-style repetitions in half time or full time of shimmies and undulations in different dance positions.	11- "Entrance of the Stars," Bellydance Superstars, Vol. 2
Assessment (optional): Students perform the culminating activity without the teacher. Teacher may prompt. Advance students may lead.	

5. Cool-down & Stretch

Perform fluid movements, review dance positions and do final stretches.	12- "Desert Twilight," Fire Dance

6. Thank and praise your students

Promote a future class, community event, or say something about the topic of the next class. Wish them a wonderful evening, weekend or week, whichever is appropriate.

Reflections:

What went well?

What could have been better?

Did the students' learning behaviors match your expectations?

What would you do differently next time?

Teaching Tip #30

While overcorrection can be a negative experience for students, so is being ignored or not corrected at all. Be sure to notice and remark on each student's effort and progress at least once (and hopefully more) during the session. If you have a small class, every student should get noticed and his or her effort acknowledged in every class.

Week 3 or 9

Vertical Hip & Ribcage Figure 8's | Chiftitelli/Wahda Sonbati & Alternative Rhythms| Exploring Fluidity & Flair

Teaching Objectives:

- Engage students in conditioning the obliques and abdominals for figure 8 movements body movements to gain body awareness, fluidity and core flexibility
- Guide students in understanding the musicality and transitions of these movements with different rhythms and musical forms
- Encourage and challenge students to explore the movements with their own flair

Key Isolations & Movements:	Chiftitelli or Wahda Sonbati Rhythm:	Aesthetics:
• Hip slide • Pelvic/hip tilt (weight-centered) • Hip lift (weight-shifted) • Ribcage lift • Ribcage slide • Ribcage tilt • Arch and Foot flexion • Vertical hip figure 8 down to up • Vertical hip figure 8 up to down (a.k.a. maya) • Vertical ribcage figure 8 both directions	Explore movements with tempo dynamics of these 8-count rhythms: slow, slow, quick, quick, slow. Explore vertical figure 8 movements with alternative music and rhythms.	Explore fluidity and transitions from upper to lower body, size, intensity, musical styling and personal flair.

Alternate or Additional Lesson: Review of Veil Class

Spring Session (Part 2)
Week 3 or 9, continued

Procedure | Suggested Playlist

1. Introduction & Warm-up

Fast warm-up	1- "Walk Like an Egyptian," Bellydance Superstars, Vol. 2
Slow warm-up	2- "Aataba," Bellydance Superstars Vol. 4

Warm-up Isolations:
    Abdominal contraction
 	
    Chest lift, slide, twist
	3- "Lion Birds," Sensual Art of Belly Dance: Fast Rhythms

Body awareness, dance positions & muscle engagement	4- "Nai Solo," Ya Salam Ya Fahtiem

2. Stationary Exercises: Weight-Centered Figure 8's

Vertical hip figure 8: Hip slide + Hip tilt	5- "El Amor Perdido," Flamenco Arab
Vertical ribcage figure 8: Ribcage slide + Ribcage tilt	

3. Review & Practice: Vertical Figure 8 Movements

Vertical hip figure 8	6- "Serpent Arms," Sensual Art of Belly Dance: Slow Rhythms
Vertical ribcage figure 8 (one both directions)	

1-2 minute break for water, questions, or comments

4. Culminating Activity: Variations of Free-Style Figure 8's

Students follow the teacher in performing variations of the movements, with an emphasis on muscle engagement. **Assessment (optional):** Students perform key parts of the drill choreography without the teacher. Teacher may prompt. Advance students may lead.	7- "Chiftitelli Unplugged," Tribal Dance Tribal Drums
	8- "Istanbul by Night," Desert Passage

5. Final Activity

Review and practice culminating activity from week 2 Add veil with simple maneuvers if appropriate.	9- "Entrance of the Stars," Bellydance Superstars, Vol. 2

6. Cool-down & Stretch

Perform fluid movements, review dance positions and do final stretches.	10- "Desert Twilight," Fire Dance

7. Thank and praise your students.

Promote a future class, community event, or say something about the topic of the next class. Wish them a wonderful evening, weekend or week.

Reflections:

What went well?

What could have been better?

Did the students' learning behaviors match your expectations?

What would you do differently next time?

Teaching Tip #31

Reward your dedicated students. Keep attendance cards and at the end of the session, award a certificate of achievement to those with perfect attendance. Students are responsible for signing in, not you. After a few sessions, those who have the fewest absences may be rewarded with a free workshop, private lesson or another item of value.

Week 4 or 10

Grapevine Step, Turns | Wahda & Waltz Rhythms | Veil Dancing & Group Formations

Teaching Objectives:

- Prepare students to perform traveling steps and turns safely with exercise to condition the feet and legs
- Engage students in spatial awareness through stepping patterns and stage formations in a defined space
- Introduce students to the flavor of Waltz-inspired Middle Eastern rhythms
- Challenge students to perform the step combinations with veil maneuvers (optional)

Key Isolations & Movements:	Suggested Combination: Combination 2:	Floor Patterns & Directions:
• Abdominal Contraction • Chest lift • Ribcage tilt and slide • Glute contraction • Horizontal hip figure 8 (front to back) • Horizontal ribcage figure 8 (front to back) **Steps:** • Grapevine	Grapevine R over L 8cts Pause 8cts, dancer's movement choice Repeat L over R For added challenge, perform combinations with veil.	Group Circle Stage Formation, "Soul Train"

Spring Session (Part 2)
Week 4 or 10, continued

Procedure | Suggested Playlist

1. Introduction & Warm-up

Procedure	Suggested Playlist
Fast warm-up	1- "Walk Like an Egyptian," Bellydance Superstars, Vol. 2
Slow warm-up	2- "Aataba," Bellydance Superstars Vol. 4

Warm-up Isolations:
    Abdominal contraction
    Ribcage lift, slide, twist
    Arm circles
	3- "Lion Birds," Sensual Art of Belly Dance: Fast Rhythms

Body awareness, dance positions & muscle engagement Explore ending poses for the finale of a dance number	4- "Nai Solo," Ya Salam Ya Fahtiem

2. Stationary Exercises: Weight-Centered Isolations

Procedure	Suggested Playlist
Hip slide Hip tilt	5- "Maksoum," Arabic Rhythms
Glute contraction Hip sway	6- "Bring it down," SharQui Workout

Select movements to review:
    Hip lift
    Hip drop
    Vertical hip figure 8
    Vertical ribcage figure 8
	7- "Awal Suhur," Musica Arabe Instrumental Vol. 7

1-2 minute break for water, questions, or comments

4. Introduce New Combinations: Grapevine Step

Introduce grapevine step and practice both directions.	8- "Wahda Sogaraya," Base and Variations) [feat. Khamis Henkesh]
Practice grapevine step combinations to wahda and walz rhythms.	9- "Tawil or Wahda Clasical Rhythm," Arab Rhythmology
8 cts grapevine step	10- "Walz 3/4," Rhythm Identification
8 cts pause and perform any movement in place, dancer's choice	11- "Walz 3/4," Rhythm Identification
Repeat to other side	

5. Culminating Activity: Grapevine Combinations in Group Formation

Guide students to perform grapevine step in a group circle formation. Perform the new combination in a circle with or without veil:
 	
   8 cts grapevine travel clockwise
 	
   8 cts stationary movement
 	
   Repeat counter clockwise
 	
Assessment (optional): Students perform the activity without the teacher. Teacher may prompt. Advance students may lead.
	12- "Darigh Nur," Mario Kirlis Junto a Saida

6. Final Activity

Review and practice the stage traveling activity from week 2. Add veil with simple maneuvers if appropriate.	13- "Entrance of the Stars," Bellydance Superstars, Vol. 2

Spring Session (Part 2)
Week 4 or 10, continued

5. Cool-down & Stretch

Perform fluid movements, review dance positions and do final stretches.	14- "Desert Twilight," Fire Dance

6. Thank and praise your students.

Promote a future class, community event, or say something about the topic of the next class. Wish them a wonderful evening, weekend or week.

Reflections:

What went well?

What could have been better?

Did the students' learning behaviors match your expectations?

What would you do differently next time?

Teaching Tip #32

If you have gained confidence with correcting students, be aware of how you're correcting and who. Take care not to target any one or two students consistently, Even if they constantly need correction, try not to single them out. Overcorrecting or targeting only certain students can lead to frustration, and the perception of favoritism, which completely block learning and toxic to a positive learning environment. Be patient, stay positive and consider each individual student's goals and abilities when offering personal attention.

Week 5 or 11

Dynamic Traveling & Combinations | Contemporary Belly Dance Music | Stage Dynamics & Floor Patterns

Teaching Objectives:

- Engage students in the dynamics of rhythmic traveling with musicality
- Prepare students to use traveling steps in group formations and floor patterns
- Provide opportunity for students to practice to stage skills in the group formations presented, ie. Soul Train, and/or traveling group circle

Key Isolations & Articulations:	Musicality of Contemporary Styling:	Stage Dynamics & Floor Patterns:
• Hip slide • Chest lift • Shoulder shimmy **Steps:** • Step-pivot • Two-step lateral travel • Side-step lateral travel	**Combination 1** Three step hip sway 4cts Three-step turn Repeat to other side **Combination 2:** 8cts Two-step lateral travel with chest lift, abdominal contract or both, ie. alternating 8cts side-step with vertical hip figure 8 Repeat to other side	Diagonal steps w/DS foot Diagonal travel, DS and UP Circular/spiral floor pattern

Spring Session (Part 2)
Week 5 or 11, continued

Procedure | Suggested Playlist

1. Introduction & Warm-up

Fast warm-up	1- "Walk Like an Egyptian," Bellydance Superstars, Vol. 2
Slow warm-up	2- "Aataba," Bellydance Superstars Vol. 4

Warm-up Isolations:
  Abdominal contraction
  Ribcage lift, slide, twist
  Arm circles
	3- "Lion Birds," Sensual Art of Belly Dance: Fast Rhythms

Body awareness, dance positions & muscle engagement Explore ending poses for the finale of a dance number	4- "Nai Solo," Ya Salam Ya Fahtiem

2. Stationary Exercises: Muscle Engagement & Isolations

Hip slide Hip tilt Glute contraction	5- "Bring it Down," The SharQui Workout
Ribcage slide, circle Ribcage figure 8 Shoulder isolations Arm circles	6- "Streams on the Nile," Ahla Leila
Shimmy practice	7- "Eshta," Raks Zahra

1-2 minute break for water, questions, or comments

3. Introduce & Practice Key Steps

Step-pivot Three-step turn Two-step lateral travel Side-step lateral travel	8- "Baladi," (7:27 version) Tribal Dance Tribal Drums

4. New Combinations: Add Movements to Steps

Three-step hip sway, three-step turn Two-step lateral travel with chest lift, side-step with figure 8	9-"Awal Suhur," Musica Arabe Instrumental Vol. 7

5. Culminating Activity: Traveling Combinations & Floor Patterns

Modeling the teacher, students perform the combinations or may dance free-style in Soul Train stage formation, two-by-two. **Assessment (optional):** Students perform the activity one by one.	10- "Darigh Nur," Mario Kirlis Junto a Saida

5. Final Activity (optional)

Review the stage activity from week 2. Add veil if appropriate.	11- "Entrance of the Stars," Bellydance Superstars Vol. 2

6. Cool-down & Stretch

Review dance positions and do final stretches	12- "Desert Twilight," Fire Dance

7. Thank and praise your students

Promote a future class, community event, or say something about the topic of the next class. Wish them a wonderful evening, weekend or week, whichever is appropriate.

Reflections:

What went well?

What could have been better?

Did the students' learning behaviors match your expectations?

What would you do differently next time?

Teaching Tip #33

Train your students and remind them in every class to stand in theirs spots in a scattered formation. This habit ensures everyone has ample room to move their arms, step side-to-side, and move forward and back. When it's time to learn choreography positions, they will already be familiar with the scattered formation. The two-row scattered formation easily transitions into a circle when it's time to travel in a circular floor pattern.

Week 6 or 12

Stage Formations | Structured Free-Style Group Dance

Teaching Objectives:

- Prepare students to perform traveling steps with specific traveling paths around the "stage"
- Provide the opportunity for students to practice movements and steps they have learned to express themselves in a safe and encourage environment
- Introduce students to the concept of improvisation

Essential Review:	Structured Improvisational or Choreography Activity:	Stage Floor Pattern:
• Stage directions • Floor pattern for "Soul Train" formation • Choose three Traveling steps • Choose four standing movements or combinations • Choose a few veil maneuvers to review • Dance positions modified for finale poses	Students form a semi-circle US and take turns on stage solo or with a classmate. Enter from upstage center with a traveling step forward. Pause to perform a standing movement or combination for 16 – 32 counts (or as little as they like). Students exit SL or SR, filing back into the semi circle line. Repeat as many times as desired. Students may opt to use veil.	"Soul Train" formation

Procedure | Suggested Playlist

1. Introduction & Warm-up

Fast warm-up	1- "Walk Like an Egyptian," Bellydance Superstars, Vol. 2
Slow warm-up	2- "Aataba," Bellydance Superstars Vol. 4

Warm-up Isolations:
   Abdominal contraction
   Ribcage lift, slide, twist
   Arm circles
	3- "Lion Birds," Sensual Art of Belly Dance: Fast Rhythms

Poses: Explore different poses that would be suitable for a finale or photo opportunity.	4- "Nai Solo," Ya Salam Ya Fahtiem

2. Stationary Exercises: Muscle Engagement & Key Movements

Hip slide Hip tilt Glute contraction	5- "Bring it Down," The SharQui Workout
Undulations Ribcage slide, circle Ribcage figure 8 Shoulder isolations Arm circles	6- "Streams on the Nile," Ahla Leila
Shimmy practice	7- "Eshta," Raks Zahra

1-2 minute break for water, questions, or comments

3. Review & Practice Key Steps

Step-pivot Three-step turn Two-step lateral travel with chest lift Side-step lateral travel with figure 8 Three-step with hip sway	8- "Baladi," (7:27 version) Tribal Dance Tribal Drums

4. Review Select Combinations & Veil Maneuvers

Select a few combinations from previous lessons to review.	9-"Awal Suhur," Musica Arabe Instrumental Vol. 7
If appropriate, select a few veil combinations or maneuvers to review.	10- "Tribal Dream," Bellydance Superstars Vol. 3

5. Culminating Activity: Structured Improvisation Activity

Model the improvisational activity for students and direct them to follow your lead, as you provide verbal cues. Encourage students to take as little as 8 counts or as much as 32 counts in the spotlight. Choose a fun song of ample length. When you sense the end of the song step in to direct students in a finale step or shimmy, and end in pose. **Assessment (optional):** Students perform the activity without teacher cues.	11- "Entrance of the Stars," Bellydance Superstars Vol. 2

6. Cool-down & Stretch

Perform fluid movements, review dance positions and do final stretches.	12- "Desert Twilight," Fire Dance

7. Thank and praise your students.

Promote a future class, community event, or say something about the topic of the next class. Wish them a wonderful evening, weekend or week.

Reflections:

How did the session go for you?

What did you learn about your students?

What would you do differently next time?

Reminders!

- Review rhythm structures before introducing the step combinations when it is relevant to the movement pattern.
- Introduce and practice movements and combinations on both sides of the body and in both directions to avoid developing muscle imbalances.
- Take short stretch breaks after every 2 to 3 songs or between sections
- Check for understanding often and pay close attention to students with known injuries.

4

Summer Session:
Specialty Topics

As summer is a time for vacations, it is a good time to have a more relaxed approach to your classes by offering a drop-in format and specialty workshops, free from the rigors of a progressive curriculum.

To create your summer drop-in session, simply select lessons from the thematic units. I would suggest corresponding the week number of your summer session to the week # of the selected lesson in the thematic units. For example, for week 1 of your summer session, select a lesson from week 1 or 7 of any unit.

Alternatively, you can combine the ideas of different lessons to create a series of individually themed classes. For a six to eight week summer session, offer two classes per theme to explore the topic.

Suggested Themes for Summer Drop-In Session

Waves & Undulations: Upper and lower body undulation, full body undulation, hand undulation, snake arms

Circles, Spirals and Eights: Horizontal hip circle and figure 8's, pelvic circle, vertical hip figure 8's, circular and spiral floor patterns

Shimmies & Vibrations: 4/4 shimmy half time, full time, double time, quadruple time, weighted and unweighted shimmies and vibrations

Traveling Hips: Combine three or four step variations with different hip movements

Specialty workshops are a great way to enhance and supplement the regular class curriculum during the summer months. By having the bulk of your specialty workshops in the summer, you can continue to keep students interested while having a more flexible schedule.

If you do not specialize in the workshop topics suggested, or you would rather not teach these topics, bring in guest instructors, or brainstorm ideas for workshops of topics you would like to offer.

Suggested Topics for Summer Workshops

"Veiled Expressions"

In the spring session, you introduced students to veil dancing. They now have an idea what it is and may be interested in learning more.

>**Pre-requisite for students:** none
>
>**Objective:** Students will learn about veil dancing as an essential element of modern belly dance.
>
>**Content:**
>
>- Conditioning the body to prepare for veil dancing
>- How to hold the veil and handle the veil in motion
>- How to use the veil to frame and highlight your movements
>- Basic veil maneuvers and technique
>- Making veil sculptures, or shapes in the air
>- Creating drama and developing dance confidence through veil work

"Raqs al Assaya: Women's Egyptian Stick Dance"

In the fall session, you introduce students to the folkloric foundations of belly dance. In this workshop they will learn how to work with an authentic folkloric prop. Those who participate in the fall session learn about saidi style steps and rhythms. For new students this is a great introduction to folkloric dancing.

Pre-requisite for students: none

Objective: Students will learn about Egyptian folkloric dance as an essential element and foundation of modern belly dance.

Content:

- Conditioning exercises to prepare the hands for twirling the cane
- How to hold the cane and handle the cane in motion
- How to frame movements with the cane
- Basic cane maneuvers and twirling technique
- Basic saidi-style steps and combinations with the cane

"Drum Solo Technique & Musicality"

Throughout the curriculum, rhythms are an integral part of the class experience. In this workshop they will learn about drum solo interpretation through your favorite concepts, combinations or choreography.

Pre-requisite for students: none

Objective: Students will learn about Arabic rhythms and tabla sounds through the drum solo as an essential element of the belly dance show.

Content:

- Conditioning exercises to prepare the body for vigorous movement
- How to hold listen to the sounds of the drum solo
- How to interpret the sounds into movements
- Basic hip and shimmy technique for drum solos
- Favorite steps and combinations or choreography for drum solo (modified for different levels)

"Balancing Props"

Each session of the curriculum begins with a thorough review and practice of the fundamental isolations and movements of Oriental belly dance. In this workshop, students will have the opportunity to further refine their isolation skills with learning how to work with a prop.

Pre-requisite for students: none

Objective: Students will learn how to balance a prop on the head as a specialty talent developed for a belly dance show.

Content:

- Preparing the item to be balanced (sword, tray, etc.)
- Posture and alignment for proper balance and coordination
- History and background of the selected prop(s)
- Basic technique for isolations and steps presented
- Favorite steps and combinations or choreography for the selected prop (modified for different levels)

"Finger Cymbals"

As music is an integral part of the dance, basic finger cymbal concepts can help students better understand rhythm and musical phrasing. In this workshop, students have the opportunity to become introduced to a traditional musical instrument that is associated with "old school" as well as modern belly dance, through your favorite combinations or choreography with cymbals.

Pre-requisite for students: none

Objective: Students will learn about finger cymbal technique and concepts as a tool for understanding essential rhythms of folkloric and modern belly dance.

Content:

- Conditioning exercises to prepare the hands for playing the cymbals
- How to hold and strike the cymbals to create different sounds
- How to hold the arms and hands while playing
- Basic finger cymbal patterns
- Favorite combinations with cymbals (modified for different levels)

"Folkloric Flavors"

In the fall session, you introduce students to the folkloric foundations of belly dance. In this workshop they will learn about two or more folkloric style dances from different regions of the Middle East. This is a great opportunity to introduce students to different cultural flavors from which modern belly dance is derived.

Pre-requisite for students: none

Objective: Students will learn about two or more of your favorite folkloric or regional dance styles that have influenced the evolution of belly dance.

Content:

- Background and history of the dance's geographic and cultural origin (brief)
- Associated rhythms, instruments and musical elements
- Typical clothing or costumes associated with the style (visual aids)
- Conditioning exercises to prepare the body for vigorous movement
- Basic characteristic steps, movements and combinations

Resources

The following pages are a collection of resources to support the themes and topics of this curriculum guide, which you can share with students.

Suggested Music Albums and Artists

Ahla Leila, Muhammad Sultan

Amarain, Amr Diab

Arab Rhythmology, Mizan Project

Arabic Jukebox, Various Artists

Arabic Rhythms, Bobby Bethoney

Arabic World Dances, Raffi Avakian

Art of the BellyDance, Voyager Records

Aziza Raqs, Various Artists

Bal Anat, Suhaila Salimpour

Belly Dance Music, Belly Dance

Bellydance Superstars Volume 2, Various Artists

Bellydance Superstars Volume 3, Various Artists

Bellydance Superstars Volume 4, Various Artists

Bellydance Superstars Volume 5, Various Artists

Beyond the Desert: Classical Egyptian Belly Dance Music, Sami Nossair Orchestra

The Dancing Drum: Volume 1, Issam Houshan

Desert Passage, Various Artists

Desert Roses and Arabian Rhythm Volume 3, Various Artists

Drum Rhythms for Oriental Dance with Mohammed "Bibo" Gaber

Drumspyder, The Nekyia Vol. 1

Fate, Susu Pampanin

Fire Dance, Omar Faruk Tekbilek and Brian Keene

Flamenco Arabe 1 and 2, Hossam Ramzy Rafa El Tachuela

The Goddess Workout, Dolphina

Hatshepsut and Other Dances, Abed Halabi and Abdel Hazim

Jalilah's Raks Sharki, Volume 6: In a Beirut Mood, Ihsan Al Munzer

Junto a Saida, Mario Kirlis

Middle Eastern Dance, 30 Hits of Belly Dance, Various Artists

Music from the Goddess Workout, Dolphina

Musica Arabe Instrumental Volume 7, Mario Kirlis

Nourhan's Raqs Sharqi I, Aboudi Badawi

Oriental Belly Dance Vol. 2, Darbouka & Tabla

Pulse of the Sphynx, The Henkesh Brothers

Raks Zahra, Michael Cox

Raqs Ayoub, Bassam Ayoub

Repercussion, Ziad Islambouli

Rough Guide to Belly (First Edition), Various Artists

Rhythm Identification, Susu Pampanin

Rhythms of Oriental Dance, Nesma

Secrets of the Eye, Hossam Ramzy

Sensual Art of Belly Dance: Fast Rhythms, Ron Wagner

Sensual Art of Belly Dance: Slow Rhythms, Ron Wagner

The SharQui Workout, Oreet

Todos Los Ritmos Arabes, Brandan Osvaldo el Beryewe

Tribal Dance Tribal Drums, Helm

Ya Salam Ya Fahtiem, George Fadel

Fall Session: Foundations in Folklore

Music

Drill Routines
Balady rhythm
"Al a Nar," Sami Nossair Orchestra
"The Arabic Party," Darbouka & Tabla, Oriental Belly Dance Vol. 2

Choreography
Option 1: "Saidi Ya Wad," Samir Srour (Soheir Zaki music), Cairo Plus
Option 2: "Move Your Belly," Dancer's Odyssey

Web Resources

***"Folkloric Dances"* by Jasmin Jahal (article):**
http://www.jasminjahal.com/articles/01_06_folkloric.html

***"The Thinking Gals Guide to Belly Dance Styles Part 3: Folkloric Dances"* by Princess Farhana (blog post):**
http://princessraqs.blogspot.com/2011/04/thinking-gals-guide-to-belly-dance_24.html

***"Belly Dance Styles: Egyptian Saidi and Raks Assaya"* by Lauren Haas (article):** http://www.bellydancestuff.com/styles-saidi.html

Book

You Asked Aunt Rocky: Answers & Advice About Raqs Sharqi & Raqs Shaabi
Morocco (C. Varga Dinicu). ISBN: 978-0-983-0690-4-1

Winter Session: Music & Choreography

Music for Choreography

"Zeina," available on:
- Belly Dance Superstars, Vol. 1 (preferred version)
- Aziza Raks
- 10 Songs Every Belly Dancer Should Know

"Snake Dance," (Version of Zeina) available on:
  Bal Anat: In the Beginning (Suhaila Salimpour)

Web Resources

"Who's Who – Mohamed Abdel Wahab" by Jasmin Jahal (article):
http://www.jasminjahal.com/articles/00_12_wahab.html

Book

Images of Enchantment
Edited by Sherifa Zuhur. ISBN: 978-9774-2446-7-4

Legends of Arabic Music

Om Kalthoum

Born: December 30, 1898
Died: February 3, 1975

Famous works include:
  "Ana Fi Intizarak" (I'm Waiting For You)
  "Alf Layla We Layla" (One Thousand and One Nights)
  "Enta Omri" (You Are My Life)
  "Enta el Hob" (You Are the Love)

Interesting fact: *"The Voice of Egypt," her songs are known for their melancholy love themes. Though sometimes the music can seem upbeat and happy, they are not happy songs. (Wikipedia.com)*

Abdel Halim Hafez

Born: June 21, 1929
Died: March 30, 1977

Famous works include:
"Ahwak" (I Adore You/I Want You)
"Zay el Hawa" (Like the Wind)
"Sawwah" (Wanderer)
"Gana el Hawa" (The Mood Struck Us)

Interesting fact: *He is among the most popular Arab singers of all time. He was also an actor, composer and movie producer. His music is still enjoyed today throughout the Arab world. (Wikipedia.com)*

Mohamad Abdel Wahab

Born: March 13, 1902
Died: May 4, 1991

Famous works include:
"Enta Omri" (sung by Om Kaltohum)
"Enta el Hob" (sung by Om Kalthoum)
"Msafer Wahdak" (Lonely Traveler)
"Zeina" (feminine name meaning beautiful one)

Interesting fact: *He was the most prolific Arab composer of his time and wrote many songs for Om Kalthum. His orchestrations combined Arabic music with Western musical forms and instruments. (al-mashriq.net)*

Farid al Atrashe

Born: October 19, 1910
Died: December 26, 1974

Famous works include:
"Habeena" (Love Me/Love Us)
"Gamil Gamal" (Beautiful Lady)
"Ya Zahratan fi Khayali" (You Appear in My Imagination)
"Awal Hamsa" (First Whisper)

Interesting fact: *He was a singer, composer, actor and virtuoso oud player. He starred in 31 Egyptian musical films, many with the famous dancer, Samia Gamal. (Wikipedia.com)*

Spring Session: Performance Skills

Music for Stage Exploration

"Entrance of the Stars," Bellydance Superstars Volume 2

"Ahla Layla," Muhammad Sultan Orchestra

Web Resources

"The Marvelous Meanderings of Morocco"
www.casbahdance.org

"Dance of the Seven Veils" by Shira
www.shira.net/sevenveils

"Lost in Translation: Fusion Confusion" by Marion Nowak
www.gildedserpent.com/cms/2011/01/13/marion-fusion-lost-in-translation/#axzz3YvAqukxN

Thrive and Soar

www.ingramcontent.com/pod-product-compliance
Lightning Source LLC
Chambersburg PA
CBHW080345300426
44110CB00019B/2510